ORAGE

DO NOT REMOVE
CARDS FROM POCKET

OPPORTUNITIES IN
CRAFTS CAREERS

Marianne Forrester Munday

Foreword by
Judith Brossart
Editor
Crafts magazine

VGM Career Horizons
a division of *NTC Publishing Group*
Lincolnwood, Illinois USA

Cover Photo Credits:

Clockwise from top left: Photo Network; Kentucky Guild of Artists and Craftsmen; Textile Arts Center; Fashion Institute of Technology.

Library of Congress Cataloging-in-Publication Data

Munday, Marianne Forrester.
    Opportunities in crafts careers / Marianne Munday.
      p. cm. — (VGM opportunities series)
    Includes bibliographical references.
    ISBN 0-8842-4068-0 (hard) — ISBN 0-8442-4069-9 (soft)
    1. Handicraft—Vocational guidance—United States. I. Title.
II. Series
TT149.M86
745′.023973—dc20
                                         93 -17351
                                             CIP

Published by VGM Career Horizons, a division of NTC Publishing Group.
© 1994 by NTC Publishing Group, 4255 West Touhy Avenue,
Lincolnwood (Chicago), Illinois 60646-1975 U.S.A.
All rights reserved. No part of this book may be reproduced, stored
in a retrieval system, or transmitted in any form or by any means,
electronic, mechanical, photocopying, recording or otherwise, without
the prior permission of NTC Publishing Group.
Manufactured in the United States of America.

3 4 5 6 7 8 9 0 VP 9 8 7 6 5 4 3 2 1

ABOUT THE AUTHOR

Marianne Forrester Munday received her B.A. from Rutgers University and an M.B.A. from Virginia Tech. She is also the author of *Opportunities in Word Processing,* published by VGM Career Horizons in 1991.

ACKNOWLEDGMENTS

The author would like to express her appreciation to each of the individuals and organizations mentioned in this book for their assistance in its preparation.

Special thanks go to Bill Forrester, who was instrumental in researching and writing the chapters on woodworking and ceramics, and to Jim Munday, who typed and edited the manuscript and offered valuable ideas and comments throughout the course of its development.

FOREWORD

Opportunities for a full-time career, supplementing a family income, or just making "pin" money in the crafts field are many and varied. As the editor of the leading how-to crafts consumer magazine, I have the pleasure of dealing daily with people in all walks of crafts and crafting.

These opportunities range from the manufacturer who produces or imports the supplies to the wholesaler who gets them into the hands of the retailer who in turn sells them to the consumer. Falling in between those three key people are the designer/author who creates designs and patterns and writes the step-by-step instructions for the kit manufacturer or the publisher and his or her team of experts to the all-important photographer, typesetter, color separator, and printer.

Let's not forget the teacher/demonstrator in a craft retail store or on the floor of a trade show. Equally visible are the self-publishers of softcover "floppy" books, the craft sellers at craft fairs, small business people who sell their patterns or specialty supplies by mail order, and crafters who sell their one-of-a-kind or limited edition projects on consignment to craft and gift shops.

The serious craft opportunist can learn much from a consumer how-to magazine. The very factors which motivate our readers to take the time to learn the skills necessary to master any given craft technique can easily be translated to the individual who doesn't have the time, patience, work space, or opportunity to make his or her own creations, but who, nevertheless, wants to enjoy and appreciate the functional uses and beauty of a well-executed handcrafted item.

No matter which avenue of crafts you decide to pursue, it is important to have a working knowledge of your audience and to channel your activities to the needs and desires of that audience. Therefore, you should be aware that most people who craft for themselves do so for the following reasons: (1) gift giving, (2) home decor, (3) holidays, (4) wearable art, and (5) pride in saying, "I made it myself" or in owning a fine-crafted, high-quality item.

If you target your craft goals to fulfilling one or several of the above needs and couple them with the love and satisfaction of a job well done, you will discover one of the most rewarding paths of endeavor you will ever experience.

Judith Brossart
Editor
Crafts magazine
PJS Publications, Inc.

To Jim

CONTENTS

What are crafts? The history of crafts in the United
States. Deciding to begin a craft career. Finding
your niche in crafts. Education. Career futures in
crafts.

Woodworking through the ages. Timber. Multipur-
pose uses for wood. The craftperson's tools. Tool
care and use. The wood industry. Woodworking careers. What to do next.

Ceramics: technology from the ancients. Improve-
ments through time. The properties of clay. Firing.
Ceramics: types and character. The ceramic artist.
Working with ceramics. From hobby to career: an

interview with a ceramic artist. Ceramic uses in industry. Ceramic engineers. Scientists and engineers: utilizing an ancient technology. Other careers in ceramics. What to do next.

CHAPTER 1

CAREERS IN CRAFTS

The crafts renaissance of a few years ago created not just a boom in the field but an explosion of new ideas and opportunities for self-styled artisans and young entrepreneurs. With new materials, advanced technology tools, and bright, innovative ideas, the crafts "field" is now a full fledged industry. Whole stores are now devoted to nothing but crafts materials, with chains opening around the country catering to the self-employed artists and craftspeople flooding the industry.

The crafts market has now forged its own niche in an old territory of gifts and collectibles, previously reserved for flea markets and shopping mall gimmicks. Today, craft fairs, shops, and galleries can be found in virtually every area of the country. Craft associations and organizations are boasting larger memberships than ever before. Many colleges and universities now offer crafts-related courses and even degrees.

The interest in crafts is often traced to our society's basic disenchantment with mass-produced goods and the individual's desire for greater self-expression. In our machinery-driven society, crafts offer both artisans and the general public an outlet for their individuality and creative talent.

It has been estimated that in the United States alone, at least one out of every two Americans age sixteen and older engages in some type of craft activity. One study indicates that this interest in crafts is growing at an annual rate of at least 20 percent. These figures are not surprising when you take into account the increasing number of hobbyists, full-time and part-time professionals, and buyers or collectors who are actively involved in craft pursuits.

Because the American public's enthusiasm for crafts is at an all-time high, career opportunities in the crafts field are greater than ever before. The result is that substantial numbers of craft enthusiasts are considering craft career alternatives, and the bottom line is that many of them are deciding to enter the field on a professional basis.

Today thousands of craft professionals make all or part of their living through their work, and that work has a ready market in a large number of craft outlets. These outlets include craft fairs, retail shops, mail order catalogs, and institutions such as hotels and restaurants, corporations, schools, and the government. Together, these markets and others have helped to make crafts a multi-billion dollar industry in the United States. The craft marketplace is discussed in more detail in Chapter 8.

It is important to point out that the crafts boom has generated a variety of interesting career options in addition to the obvious one of actually producing handcrafted pieces. There is also a very real demand for craft dealers, show and fair organizers, materials suppliers, teachers, writers, and lecturers, among others. Crafts-related careers are discussed in more detail in Chapters 5 and 6.

As we journey through the world of crafts, it should become evident that opportunities in the crafts field are limited only by your talent, creativity, enthusiasm, and business sense. With these basic characteristics, it is possible to have both a personally fulfilling and financially rewarding career in the craft marketplace.

WHAT ARE CRAFTS?

Crafts are occupations or trades that require manual dexterity and/or artistic skill. Manual dexterity points to the fact that craft items are predominantly made by hand rather than by machine. Artistic skill refers to the craftsperson's emphasis on quality, beauty, and creativity in the work's design and production.

There are many different types of crafts. Some of the most popular include ceramics, woodworking, fiber art, and metal working; there are many, many more. The following two examples—woodworking and ceramics—point to the diversity of creative possibilities and career opportunities that often exist in a given craft field.

Woodworking is one of the most widely practiced crafts in the United States today. Using wood, the craftsperson can create a seemingly endless variety of products. For example, the same piece of wood might be used to create a sculpture, a toy train, or a church pew. The ceramist, on the other hand, uses minerals of the earth to produce a vast assortment of ceramic products. For many people, the word *ceramics* conjures up images of dishes and pottery; dishes and pottery, however, represent only a very small percentage of the ceramics industry. Ceramic products also include glass, cement, insulators, building materials, and abrasives.

Craft products fall into two general categories: one-of-a-kind items and production items. *One-of-a-kind designs* are individual craft pieces that are not easily copied or reproduced. That is, they are unique, original works of art. Many craftspeople prefer to create one-of-a-kind, high quality crafts because they are true expressions of individuality and talent. Unfortunately, high costs of production and the huge commitment of time necessary to make one-of-a-kind pieces prohibit the majority of craft artisans from concentrating on such designs. However, a small percentage of craftspeople have been successful at making a living from their one-of-a-kind creations. These individuals have been fortunate enough to find a profitable market for a small number of high quality, often expensive craft pieces.

Most craftspeople make the bulk of their living by producing a number of similar craft items that are based on a common mold or design. Such pieces are generally known as *production items*. Production items can be made much more quickly and much less expensively than one-of-a-kinds. As a result, the craftsperson can produce a larger number of items and sell them at a much lower price; this greatly expands the potential market.

Ideally, the craftsperson has the time and talent to produce both categories of crafts. Some have been able to successfully produce unique, one-of-a-kind pieces on a small scale while also turning out a larger number of production items to support themselves.

THE HISTORY OF CRAFTS IN THE UNITED STATES

The roots of our current craft movement can be traced to colonial times. Our country's first settlers included woodworkers, blacksmiths, weavers, and potters who crossed the Atlantic and settled down to make a living working at their individual crafts. In their day-to-day work, these craft professionals exemplified what has become a longstanding American tradition of hard work and skilled hands.

Beginning in the nineteenth century and continuing into the twentieth, craft work began to decline in importance in the United States. One major reason for this decline was the onset of the Industrial Revolution. With the mass introduction of power-driven machinery, most products could suddenly be made faster and much more cheaply by machine than by hand. Americans could now purchase a vast array of goods that was never available to them before; they quickly became obsessed with machines and technology. The age of mass production set in, and in the process, interest in crafts rapidly declined.

However, during this time period the craft movement did not die. In virtually every area of the country, small groups of dedicated men and women continued to support the craft tradition in spite of the emergence of mass-produced goods. For example, a group of socially prominent young women, excited by advances in the ceramics field, started a number of pottery clubs that nurtured the American pottery movement. Several states maintained craft associations, some of them very prosperous, and a number of craft magazines, including *Handicraft* and *The Craftsman,* began publication.

In the early 1900s, crafts programs began to find their way into schools of higher learning. In 1901 Alfred University in Alfred, New York, opened the first school of clay work. Similar programs were soon adopted at other schools around the country.

In 1943 the American Craft Council (A.C.C.) was founded by Alleen Osborn Webb. This national organization, still a powerful force in the craft movement, became a major advocate of and source of support for American craftspeople. The A.C.C. is profiled in detail in Appendix B.

Following World War II, the American people slowly began to renew their interest in crafts. A more technologically aware population started to examine the quality of machine-produced goods and to once again appreciate the beauty of handcrafted pieces. Colleges continued to increase their crafts-related offerings, and a whole generation started to be reintroduced to the crafts field.

It wasn't until the 1960s, however, that evidence of a coming crafts boom began to materialize. Some Americans, disenchanted with the excesses brought about by the technological age, began to lead a more natural lifestyle. One important offshoot of this new lifestyle was a renewed interest in things made by hand.

Some people began learning craft skills and producing crafts; others began buying craft items.

By the 1970s it was clear that American interest in crafts was more than a passing fad. Craftspeople were becoming better educated and more experienced; as a result, the quality of American crafts was rising to new heights. The public was responding by buying more crafts than ever before.

Today public interest in crafts is at an all-time high, as evidenced by the fact that crafts has become a multi-billion dollar industry. The aspiring craft professional has more career options available than ever before. The purpose of the remainder of this book is to make you aware of the broad range of opportunities that exist and to provide you with the kinds of information you need to decide if a craft career is really for you.

DECIDING TO BEGIN A CRAFT CAREER

Is a craft career really for you? Before making such an important decision, take some time to assess your individual interests, skills, and personality traits to see if they are compatible with a career in the crafts field.

There are two categories of characteristics that are necessary in order to have a personally fulfilling and financially rewarding craft career: technical skills and personal traits. *Technical skills* include those specific knowledges, skills, and abilities that are necessary to succeed as a professional in the crafts field. *Personal traits* are those individual qualities or characteristics that also contribute to your success. Take some time to review these characteristics and determine whether or not they describe you. Please note that although the following discussion centers on the producing craftsperson, these technical skills and personal traits are important for *any* position in the crafts field.

Professional Quality Skills Needed

EXPERTISE IN YOUR CRAFT

Today, more than ever before, craft professionals must be highly educated in their craft; they must maintain the willingness to learn, improve, and update their skills. Why? The crafts field is highly competitive and only the most skilled survive and prosper in the long run.

Therefore, aspiring craftspeople should concentrate on acquiring the specific knowledge and skills necessary to be proficient at their particular craft. They should attend seminars and courses related to their field of interest, read craft publications, and continuously strive to improve the quality of their work.

COMMITMENT TO QUALITY WORKMANSHIP

Because the crafts field is growing at such a fast pace, the quality of some crafts has suffered. As the public continues to become better educated regarding crafts, however, shoddy workmanship is less and less tolerated. Therefore, craft professionals must be committed to good design, quality materials, and quality workmanship in order just to be competitive.

BUSINESS SKILLS

Unfortunately, it is possible to produce a high quality product that the public wants, yet fail to sell that product because of poor business skills. If you are seriously considering crafts as a career, be sure to take the time to sharpen your business background.

It has been proven time and time again that basic business skills are essential to a successful craft operation. Therefore, all aspiring craft professionals are strongly encouraged to take business courses, including finance, management, and marketing, as well as to keep up-to-date on laws and issues that affect their practice. Today, many colleges and universities offer business courses as an integral part of their crafts curriculum. Craft students are encouraged, and often required, to take such courses.

Personal Traits

PROFESSIONALISM

In order to be successful, craft professionals must combine their creative talent with people skills and an understanding of business practices. They must be resourceful, independent, and willing to take initiative. Above all else, they must treat their customers honestly and with respect.

CREATIVITY

Creativity alone does not ensure that your product will be a success, but it certainly is a crucial ingredient in the total formula. Creativity refers to the ability to be imaginative, original, and inventive in your craft endeavors. Some of the most successful craft professionals trace their success to their ability to produce unique offerings. Their unique offerings may be the result of different materials, innovative equipment, or original designs, but it is that uniqueness that sets them apart from the rest.

ENTHUSIASM

Enthusiasm translates to wholehearted interest in both your work and your customer. If you love the crafts field more for itself than for its financial rewards, you will probably be successful. Remember, being a craft professional should be fun and should stimulate your creative juices. When that happens, the possibilities are endless.

RISK TAKING

Many employment opportunities in the crafts fields necessarily involve some degree of risk. Therefore, most people do not consider crafts a "safe" career. First of all, there is often no guaranteed paycheck each week because financial rewards are closely tied with how well your crafts are selling. In addition, many craft careers are not cozy nine-to-five, Monday-through-Friday jobs. A much larger commitment of time—including weekends and holidays—is often necessary, especially when you are new to the field. However, those who succeed generally report that they regard crafts more as a way of life than as a job; that feeling alone makes it all worthwhile.

SELF-DISCIPLINE

Self-discipline is another crucial component of success, especially for the craftsperson who is self-employed. In order to produce high quality pieces on a regular basis, the professional must impose a set of self-controls, to include a routine work schedule and production standards of acceptable vs. unacceptable work.

PATIENCE

It takes time to develop a following and to earn sufficient income from a craft. Therefore, patience—the ability to persevere despite difficulty or setbacks—is essential.

FINDING YOUR NICHE IN CRAFTS

Which craft should you learn? This is a very important decision. As you are no doubt aware, there are just too many categories of crafts to be proficient at each one. Therefore, you will want to learn the craft that best matches your individual interests and skills. The following guidelines should assist you in making an informed decision:

1. Familiarize yourself with the major categories of crafts and the various career options available in each category. Some of these options are discussed in the following chapters.
2. Do an in-depth study of those fields that are of interest to you. As you assess the relative advantages and disadvantages of each field, be sure to take into account your own background and interests.
3. Talk to individuals who are currently working in various craft fields. They should be able to answer your specific questions and to give you a realistic description of their day-to-day routine.
4. Take some time to do a complete self-assessment. In particular, seriously evaluate whether or not you have the technical and personal skills necessary for a successful career in a given craft field.

Keep in mind that a craft career is not for everyone. However, if you feel that you have what it takes, you are well on your way to becoming an important part of the exciting field of crafts.

EDUCATION

In order to be successful, today's craft professionals must be highly skilled and educated in their crafts. In addition, they must possess the business tools that are necessary in order to compete effectively in the craft marketplace. For most of us, the acquisition and fine tuning of these skills are lifelong processes.

There are a variety of ways to go about learning a particular craft. Each type of training has potential advantages and disadvantages. Therefore, you should carefully consider each option available to you and pick the one that best suits your individual circumstances.

In general, you can follow a formal course of instruction or a more traditional, informal course. A growing number of craft professionals are choosing some combination of the two.

Traditionally, interest in crafts has been guided by childhood experiences, the influence of a teacher or mentor, or other personal experiences. Certainly, the presence of crafts in the home has been found to have a very positive impact on youngsters. Over time, exposure to one or more crafts often leads to the development of interest in those crafts either as a hobby or as a vocation. Often, one person in particular acts as a mentor to an individual. That mentor may be a family member, friend, or anyone else who inspires an individual to learn a particular craft.

Apprenticeship is another very traditional means of craft education. Long before there were schools of formal education, apprenticeship was the primary way that one went about learning a particular craft. Young men (usually ages 10 to 14) would go to work for a journeyman in exchange for room and board. Little by little, they would learn the craftsperson's trade.

Today, with the resurgence of interest in crafts, apprenticeships are once again popular. Many aspiring craftspeople try to work closely with an established craft artisan in order to learn the more technical and practical details of their particular craft.

On the average, apprentices stay with their mentors for a year or less. Sometimes, the craft artist pays the apprentice a nominal fee for services; often, the apprentice pays for the privilege of working with the professional. In a small number of cases, it is possible to acquire an outside source of financial support, such as the National Endowment for the Arts.

Michael Scott, in *The Craft Business Encyclopedia,* offers some important insight into apprentice/craft professional relationships. He cautions to give careful thought to the following: 1) whether or not the craft artist and apprentice are personally compatible; 2) whether the craft artist is emotionally and psychologically equipped to teach the craft with patience and under-standing; and 3) what the specific arrangements and working conditions will be. It should be clear that one should not enter into an apprenticeship relationship without a complete under-standing of all aspects of the arrangement.

Formal education in crafts is a relatively recent development. It was not until the 1960s and 1970s that craft courses began to be readily available to the general population. Today, craft courses are offered by a wide variety of institutions, including colleges and universities, junior colleges, art schools, craft or-ganizations, vocational schools, and adult education programs. In those institutions that offer other courses in addition to crafts, it is generally reported that the craft courses are among the most popular.

Today, many successful craftspeople report that their back-ground includes a number of college courses. In fact, the trend is toward receiving a crafts-related degree. It is now possible to obtain a two-year associate's degree, four-year bachelor's degree, and even a master's degree in a crafts-related discipline.

Most craft professionals agree that a good general education is important, in addition to specific craft courses. The crafts-person must be a problem solver, and a well-rounded educa-tional background improves problem-solving skills. Therefore, if you are considering formal schooling as a means of furthering your craft education, try to include a variety of courses in your curriculum.

A growing number of schools now offer marketing, manage-ment, and finance courses that are specifically directed toward professional craftspeople. If you are interested in furthering your education in a particular craft field, be sure to consult your local library for reference sources. Following are two books that you should review:

The College Blue Book. New York: MacMillan Publishing Co., 1991. (Includes a listing of schools by subject area, including *Crafts*).

Index of Majors, 1989–90. New York: College Entrance Examination Board, 1989.

Also, take some time to visit organizations such as your local junior college, craft schools, and vocational and adult education programs. The majority of these organizations now offer crafts-related courses or can direct you to other organizations that do.

It is important to remember that a craft education is a never-ending process. Craft professionals must continue to keep abreast of new developments in their fields of interest. This can be accomplished by reading magazines and books associated with a particular field, attending pertinent lectures, registering for any new courses that are offered, and maintaining professional relationships with other craftspeople.

The bottom line is that a well-rounded, continuous education is the key to a successful craft career. Without it, the craft professional will not be equipped with the tools and information necessary to successfully operate in today's highly competitive and constantly changing marketplace.

CAREER FUTURES IN CRAFTS

Without a doubt, employment opportunities in the crafts field will continue to grow at an above average rate for the foreseeable future. Crafts has proven itself to be a strong and viable industry even in tight economic times. Public demand for crafts has skyrocketed, and this demand means a greater need than ever for quality crafts. More craftsworkers, both full time and part time, will be needed to meet that need.

CHAPTER 2

WOODWORKING CRAFTS AND CAREERS

Working with wood is, without a doubt, the most popular craft activity in the United States today. Whittling, woodcarving—even furniture making and industrial carpentry—are all crafts that give deep, enduring satisfaction to many thousands of people.

Why all the interest in wood? Why does this craft's popularity increase every year? The reasons, like wood's enthusiasts, are many. To begin with, wood is an abundant resource. Trees can be found almost all over the globe, and it seems that wherever one finds trees, one finds people, too. People have always seemed to settle by wooded areas; since wood has always been readily available, work in wood has been a natural and universal development. Different peoples throughout the world have used wood to build homes, magnificent churches, and everyday objects like cups, bowls and spoons.

Wood is an easy material to work with, and the articles that woodworkers produce are generally useful. Working in wood helps to develop hand and machine skills, as well as good safety habits. Wood enthusiasts learn about tools, good design, and the quality of wood products; they also develop creative abilities while getting to know the process of woodworking and the wood industry.

Finally, woodworkers experience the personal satisfaction that comes from planning and making something with one's own hands. An economical, strong, and versatile material, wood is and always will be essential to everyday life and to everyday people with the desire to create.

WOODWORKING THROUGH THE AGES

The earth's first craftspeople were probably woodworkers. Early on, people discovered that of all the earth's natural materials, wood was the easiest to work with. Nature has provided us for ages with a ready-to-work supply of wood around the globe. And because we can continually plant trees for use later on, wood is the world's only structural material that grows as a crop.

Society's first woodworkers were probably generalists. Using stone axes, fire, and logs, they were able to make chairs, tables, even boats or chests. These last two items were formed from partly burnt out and excavated tree trunks. A long-favored travelling receptacle, the trunk takes its name from the fact that the chest was merely a burnt-out, carved-out tree trunk with a lid.

With the discovery that fire could also be used to work iron, blacksmiths and carpenters were able to work together to make *nailed* wood furniture. Other innovations to soon follow were iron-hinged, mounted doors, boarded post houses, and planked boats. In the Middle Ages, the most important craftworker was the *joiner,* so called because the joiner developed new construction methods from ingenious ways of joining wood. These new methods meant different ways of designing furniture, staircases, and domestic and religious buildings.

Joiners supplied the artistic appeal to churches from the earliest times. During the Middle Ages and after, joiners and a subgrouping called carver-joiners were responsible for a church's benches, choir stalls, doors, pulpits, lecterns, and other items. Joiners were, in fact, ultimately responsible for the survival of early churches and great halls: their knowledge and skill allowed them to build hammer-beam roofs for these buildings that were constructed in such a way that wide spans could be bridged without putting a strong outward thrust on the walls. Many of these early churches and great halls still stand today in Europe and are still structurally sound. In fact, many of the joiner's methods of "jointing" have never been improved.

Because of a familiarity with wood's particular qualities and limitations, the joiner was able to establish different criteria for strength, which set the standards of dimensions (the viable length, width, and height) for particular constructional purposes for hundreds of years. The joiner's contributions to building during the Middle Ages are said to have inspired even the finest stone masons of the day.

Around the middle of the 1600s, new furniture crafters began plying their trade alongside the joiners. These furniture makers included chair makers, carvers, and mirror frame makers. Another expert of the period was the *turner,* who "threw" chairs on a lathe (one of the earliest, if not the earliest, woodworking machines in the world). Using this lathe, turners were able to produce furniture items faster and to add changing designs to furniture. Musical instrument makers, who also worked with wood, designed and made special tools for their unique craft; they also determined which woods had the right tonal qualities and resonance for the instrument they were making. Cofferers (who made leather-covered trunks, or "coffers"), shipwrights, wheelwrights, and coach and wagon builders all made important contributions to wood crafting. Coopers, the artisans who made or repaired wooden casks and tubs, were also highly skilled wood craftspeople. They used hooped staves to build circular or oval vessels that were too large for the turner's lathe to turn. These people were designers, fabricators, and engineers all in one, designing vessels that were strong yet graceful and made from the right variety of wood. Some craftspeople, in fact, specialized in growing trees to form particular shapes that would suit their purposes.

Trees have even provided the footwear of people throughout the ages. Soles were often made of wood. In some places, wooden clogs have been worn for centuries and are still considered fashionable today. Until the nineteenth century, women attached wooden pattens (or platforms) to their shoes to keep them out of the mud. Beech wood is still used to make heels; willow, because of its natural springiness, was used to make the feet on artificial limbs. Wood has even been tried as a road material, but the idea was abandoned because it wore down, became slick after rainfalls, swelled, splintered, and warped.

Before World War II, wood was commonly used as a floor covering. Hardwood floors are making a comeback, as new techniques of making hardwood strips and parquet floors have made prices competitive.

TIMBER

As mentioned earlier, trees are found all over the world. This is not to say, however, that trees grow everywhere. There are very specific factors that determine whether an area is suitable for the growing of specific types of trees.

In general, it is the *latitude,* not the longitude, that determines what kind of tree will or will not grow in a certain part of the world. The importance of latitude is pretty much proven by the fact that particular types of forest occur in more or less horizontal belts around the globe. Just north and south of the equator, for example, a tropical belt of hardwood forests can be found. In temperate climates north and south of the tropics, we find temperate hardwoods and a mixed hardwood/softwood belt. Further north and further south, great areas of softwoods are found. The terms "hardwood" and "softwood" are the most widely used, but they are not ideal because there are many exceptions to the accuracy of the description. In general, however, the structure of a hardwood is more complex than that of a softwood. Hardwoods are used for paneling, furniture, flooring, cabinets, musical instruments, and the like, while softwoods are used to make plywood, structural lumber, roofing, subflooring, and so on.

In temperate zones, outward-growing (or exogenous) trees provide nearly all hardwoods and softwoods. In tropical lands, inward-growing (or endogenous) trees are used for structural and decorative purposes. Exogenous trees may be divided into two main groups—hardwoods and softwoods—which are further broken down into families, genera, and species. There are more than 40,000 species of hardwood trees.

Other important factors, such as the amount of rainfall, soil fertility, pH value of the soil, wind, sun, fire, even industry, will determine if a given area will support tree life. These same factors will also determine how fast or slow a tree grows. To a person who works with wood, too-fast growth means wood of less than average strength, especially with softwoods. Slow-growing trees, on the other hand, will produce wood that is dense, hard, and heavy.

MULTIPURPOSE USES FOR WOOD

Trees have long served a number of important uses. Aside from giving us a shady spot on a sunny day or enhancing a landscape, trees have provided shelter from the elements, given protection to crops, and acted as a carving and building material for people all over the world.

Centuries of trial and error have shown that different trees have different qualities and characteristics. To do a job properly, workers in wood discovered early on that the right wood and the right tools were needed. One could not simply cut down any tree and and decide its wood would make a strong table, chair, or house. Trees are also products of their environments; years of bad weather might make a tree's wood of less-than-desirable strength or flexibility.

Like every living thing, trees grow old. As trees mature, each year's growth is gradually covered by the next year's growth. This is why, if you were to cut a tree cross-sectionally, the "years" appear as rings. Like every living thing, trees are also subject to diseases, defects, and flaws. One such defect, called *shakes*, appears as breaks in the wood's growth rings, and as vertical faults running throughout the tree structure. Knots and holes are other defects that can also render wood useless for a particular purpose: the knots can drop out, while holes may mean the wood is structurally unsound for a particular use. To test wood for holes, you can tap it with a mallet and compare the sound with the sound made on good timber of the same type. A different sound may mean different (poor) quality.

Following are some wood types and the ways they have been used throughout the centuries.

Beech

Beech is a strong, tough wood that is difficult to split when one is working with it. Beech takes paint and silver or gilt gesso well; it also stains and polishes very nicely. It has an even color of light brown, or a light pink if the wood has been steamed. Its featureless grain makes beech easy to match in joining; the wood also gives quite well. Perhaps beech's greatest disadvantage is that the wood decays quickly in a damp atmosphere.

Beech has been used to make toys, bowls, floors, mallets, tool handles, rolling pins, woodworker's bench tops, chopping blocks, even book covers. Beech was so universally used as the cover-board of early books that the German word for beech (*buche*) eventually became *buch,* or "book."

Oak

Oak is another strong, popular building material. As late as the middle of the seventeenth century, oak was used for just about everything: building, furniture, joinery, and paneling. Two centuries later would find oak the number-one material for shipbuilding; its naturally curved limbs were perfect for a ship's ribs, sterns, and sternposts. Its curved limbs were also ideal for the wooden "wishbone" frame structure of medieval houses.

Oak has been used for railroad ties, telephone poles, joinery, cabinets, and parquet, strip, and block flooring. It is also a favorite wood for sculpture and carving because of its open texture, the ease with which it splits radially, and the fact that it stains well. Woodworkers find that oak is better for large pieces than for fine work because the wood can be coarse.

High grade oak is called *wainscot oak* (the term is Old Dutch), and has been used for paneling since the sixteenth century. Because of this popular use for the wood, the paneling itself came to be called *wainscotting.*

Chestnut

Chestnut is also a popular wood for craftspeople. Chestnut is not quite as strong or durable as oak, but its same qualities and appearance (in odor and grain) make the wood almost indistinguishable from oak. Chestnut has been used for virtually all the same purposes as oak. It is also considered to be a good wood for carving.

Ash

Ash's toughness and elastic qualities make it a special purpose wood, best for sporting goods. Hockey sticks, baseball bats, tennis rackets, skis, oars, billiard cues—when sports equipment calls for strength and springiness, ash is the natural wood of choice. For years, ash was also used for wheelbarrows and handcarts because it could withstand jolts and jars. Since the wood absorbs shocks well, it also makes great handles for picks, shovels, axes, and other tools.

Sycamore

Sycamore is a quick-growing hardwood that is similar to oak, but it is softer and not quite as durable under exposure to the elements. Sycamore is a good wood for indoor housework: it saws easily and planes to a smooth, silky surface. Because of its even color and interlocked grain, this wood is very good for sculpture; the grain ensures that small, delicate features won't chip off.

Sycamore has a light color that has long made it a favorite wood for furniture. Since the wood has no taste or smell, it can be used for kitchen items. Sycamore has been used to make a number of dairy items, including churns, butter skimmers, and cheese molds. The wood has also been a favorite of violin makers, who have used it for violin sides and backs.

Maple

The maple tree is related to the sycamore, but its wood is harder and heavier. It serves all the same purposes as sycamore and will stand up to considerable punishment. This quality has made maple a favorite wood for floors and roller rinks.

Walnut

Walnut is a handsome wood that, when cut, reveals burrs, curls, and other figures that have made the wood a natural choice for good exhibition pieces. Walnut's qualities and beauty make it fine cabinet and joinery timber. In the past, walnut has been used to make church furniture and Georgian interiors.

These are just a few of the many kinds of wood and wood uses available to the woodworker. As you become more familiar with wood and more skilled in its uses, you will be able to determine which wood best suits your particular needs, whether they are whittling, carving, furniture, or house building.

THE CRAFTPERSON'S TOOLS

Just as important as using the right type of wood for a particular purpose is using the proper tools for that purpose and using the tools properly. There are literally thousands of tools for woodworking. We will discuss here just a few of the tools that may be used by a beginner in woodcrafts. As one's interest and skills grow, one can add on to this collection.

Tape Ruler. Tape rulers are usually made of flexible steel. They come in lengths of 6 feet to 10 feet and are used to measure long distances.

Scratch Awl. The scratch awl is used to mark the center for holes to be drilled or bored. It can be used to punch holes in paper, cardboard, or leather; it can also be used to punch small holes for starting nails and screws.

Try Square. The try square has a metal blade and a metal or wooden handle that are at right angles to each other, forming an "L." It is used to test the squareness of adjacent surfaces and to draw guidelines.

Hand Saw. A hand saw is used to cut wood to different shapes, lengths, and widths and to make joints to hold different pieces of a project together.

Hand Plane. A hand plane is used to smooth rough surfaces and to straighten the surface of a piece of wood.

Chisel. A chisel is a cutting tool with a sharp, beveled cutting edge. This edge is used to shape and fit parts; it should be kept very sharp.

Gouge. A gouge is a curved-bladed chisel used to shape edges or to make grooves. The gouge is struck by a mallet, which should be heavy enough to do the work for you but not too heavy to lift.

Rasps, Files, and Abrading Tools. Rasps are "grater cutters" that leave the surface of the wood with a ridged or furrowed surface for a finer finish; a file may be used to remove burrs or sharp edges; other abrading tools will smooth, shape, or form wood. If a fine smooth effect is required, further work may be done with a metal or glass scraper, and the end results may be smoothed with sandpaper.

Along with the tools just mentioned, the woodcrafter will also need a good assortment of "plain old carpenter's tools," among them drills, a workbench, wood screws, nails, wood glue, paint brushes, finishes, and vises.

TOOL CARE AND USE

Preparing Wood

It is extremely important that all the tools you use when woodworking are kept in good repair. Tools need to be very sharp, and you will probably find that you spend more time sharpening a tool than using it. However, to do a job correctly, your tools must be in top working order. A grindstone, an oilstone, and "slips" will keep your awls, flat chisels, and carving knives sharp and ready to use. Proper tool care will ensure you hours more enjoyment at your newfound hobby or career.

When using wood tools, it is also imperative that you give yourself lots of space to work with. Your work area should be large enough that you can walk completely around your project to view it from all sides. Because the tools you will be working with are extremely sharp, the area you work in should be well-lighted, and you should *always* work away from your body. The piece of wood that you are cutting, chipping, or carving should be firmly clamped to the workbench so that both your hands will be free to maneuver—and maintain total control of—your cutting tools.

Once you have selected the appropriate type of wood for your project, take some time to be sure that the wood is ready for work. The wood should be clean of dirt, paint, and foreign objects (such as old nails or pieces of wire). If you are using old lumber or a piece of wood from an old fallen tree, your inspection for these foreign objects should be particularly thorough, as they may dull (or ruin) your woodworking tools.

Be sure, too, that you plan out your work in advance. The good woodworker does not just start hacking away at a piece of wood, hoping for the best. Keep a sketch book handy. Before you start cutting or carving, draw several pictures of your project, as seen from a number of angles. Good drawing, you will find, is the essence of good carving. If the piece you are working on will be three-dimensional, you may even want to make a soap or clay carving first, so that you will have a better picture of what you are striving for.

Of course, basic woodworking techniques cannot be taught or learned from the limited introduction to the field presented here. The fine arts of woodcarving, sculpting, carpentry, and cabinet-making are best learned from careful study, patience, and lots of practice. Initially, the work will not be easy, but as you find yourself becoming more skilled in basic techniques, layout, squaring, cutting, designing, carving, etc., the end results of your labors will be extremely rewarding.

THE WOOD INDUSTRY

Centuries of use have borne out the fact that wood is an exceptionally versatile construction material. A renewable resource, wood comes in many types and strengths, is attractive, does not conduct electricity, and is easily worked. For these reasons, wood is used just about everywhere: for homes, furniture, newspapers, books, magazines, boats, sporting equipment, and musical instruments. And despite the proliferation of today's mass-produced products (like metal alloys, plastics, and rubber), wood products are far from obsolete.

Over 30 percent of the world's timberland is in the former Soviet Union countries, while about 18 percent is in North America; but both regions predominate in softwoods. Per-capita consumption of wood in the United States, however, is estimated to be three-and-a-half times that of the rest of the entire world. The United States lumber industry began in New England over three hundred years ago; today the major lumber-producing states are Washington, Oregon, California, and Idaho. It is a healthy industry. Thousands of jobs exist for woodworkers in construction, manufacturing, even forestry. The largest single skilled trade in the United States today is carpentry, but one will also find ample career opportunities in cabinetmaking, architecture, furniture design, and teaching. Let's take a closer look at some career opportunities for workers in wood.

WOODWORKING CAREERS

Carpenter

Carpenters are employed in almost every type of construction work but generally work in one particular field. Carpenters make up the largest of the building trades, playing an important role in the building of houses and other structures, making furniture, finishing interior work, doing maintenance work, and so on. Carpenters may either work for themselves or may work for a contractor or owner; some alternate between the two. Their work may take them indoors and outdoors; it involves constant physical activity throughout the day. For those carpenters working on group projects, such as a construction site, the ability to work with others and follow directions is a necessity.

People who choose carpentry for a career are good with tools, mathematics, and drawing. They can follow instructions and, from blueprints, turn a vision into a reality. Most carpenters start their training as apprentices, usually under a four-year training program. The occupation is strongly unionized and still predominated by men. Apprentices make about half the salary of journeymen (or skilled professionals). In the early 1990s union carpenters averaged a minimum hourly wage of over $11.

Carpentry is a challenging profession, offering changes in work sites, projects, and coworkers. Employment outlook: very good.

Cabinetmaker

Cabinetmakers are manufacturers of furniture. Using drawings and blueprints as planning guides, they select the proper lumber for the piece they are working on; they sketch on the lumber itself the outlines of the various parts they need. Using power saws and other woodworking machines, cabinetmakers will cut out, trim, shape, and nail or glue the parts to form a finished piece of furniture. Over 81,000 people were employed by the furniture-manufacturing industry in the early 1990s, most of whom began their employment as helpers or apprentices. While there are no special educational requirements for this field, it does help to be adept in woodworking, math, and blueprint reading.

The employment outlook for furniture manufacturers is quite good, as a shortage of skilled workers in the early part of this decade has not yet been alleviated. Beginning furniture manufacturing workers earn about $200–$300 a week, but skilled artisans do have the opportunity to make much more. Furniture makers should enjoy working with wood and working with their hands; they should also be able to stand or stoop for prolonged periods of time and be able to lift or turn heavy pieces.

Forester

Foresters are concerned with managing, developing, and protecting natural resources. They plan the growing and harvesting of trees for parks or industrial uses; they also protect trees and forest areas from disease, fire, harmful insects, and people. Foresters and conservationists will, for the most part, specialize in one area of work, but their working conditions will be extremely varied and often demanding. They are involved in outdoor work in all kinds of weather, sometimes in remote areas. Long hours fighting fires or on search-and-rescue missions will also be required.

In 1990 foresters and conservationists held about 64,000 jobs, with almost half of those positions provided by the federal government. A quarter of those jobs were with state governments and the remainder in private industry.

A bachelor's degree in forestry is the minimum educational requirement; as of 1991 over fifty colleges and universities offered bachelor's degrees or higher in forestry. Job opportunities are limited for foresters and conservationists, although some growth is predicted in the private sector, as opposed to the federal government. Foresters with a bachelor's degree earned a starting salary of between $16,973 and $21,023 a year in 1991; those with a master's degree earned between $21,023 and $25,717 or more.

Woodcarver and Sculptor

Woodcarvers and sculptors work with wood to form toys, statues, works of abstract art, and objects of lasting beauty for private and professional purposes. While no specific training in these areas is necessary, many of the techniques may be taught in high school, college, or specialty art schools. Many woodcarvers and sculptors are self-taught or have picked up the rudiments of their craft from other wood artists.

There are positives as well as negatives to a career in the arts. While no supervision is necessary after you have been trained, your public relations skills must be good, and your talent even better, if you expect to make sales. Quite often, artists do not make enough money to support themselves or their families, and so they must take a job offering steady income while they carve or sculpt in their free time. Successful woodcarvers, however, may make good money; but working for themselves, they have no benefits or vacations. For these reasons, many become teachers of their art.

Whether woodworking attracts you as a hobby or as a potential career, an exciting future awaits you working with a medium that allows you to express yourself creatively, to use math and technical skills, and to make beautiful or useful objects for yourself and for others.

WHAT TO DO NEXT

Additional information on woodworking and woodworking careers may be solicited from the following sources:

National Wood Carvers Association
    7424 Miami Avenue
    Cincinnati, Ohio 45243

United Brotherhood of Carpenters & Joiners of America
    101 Constitution Avenue N.W.
    Washington, DC 20001

Associated General Contractors of America
    1957 E Street N.W.
    Washington, DC 20006

American Forestry Association
    1516 P St. NW
    Washington, DC 20005

An extensive assortment of books on woodworking can also be found in the following catalog:

The Woodworker's Library
 R. Sorsky Bookseller
 3845 North Blackstone
 Fresno, CA 93726

Don't forget, too, the many resources that are available to you at your local public library.

CHAPTER 3

CERAMIC CRAFTS AND CAREERS

The term *ceramics* refers to the technique of molding and shaping earthy materials (usually different kinds of clay) into objects of practical or artistic value, and then permanently hardening those objects by exposing them to high temperatures. As you will see, this is a simplified definition of a craft that is nearly as old and diverse as the human race itself.

The craft of ceramics has been with us since the early Stone Age, and over time it continues to show remarkable versatility. Ceramic applications can range from the simple and practical to the ornately decorative to the complex and technical. The same basic materials and technology that have given us clay bricks, earthenware bowls, and porcelain vases may also be found in spark plugs, thermal insulation for spacecraft, nuclear reactors—even the kitchen sink. Because ceramic materials are heat-resistant, abrasive-resistant, and incredibly strong even at high temperatures, modern ceramists are continually discovering more and more about how materials from the earth can be used to make a diverse group of products that serve many different needs.

CERAMICS: TECHNOLOGY FROM THE ANCIENTS

The field of ceramics has rightfully been called our oldest technology. Our fascination with the possibilities of mud and clay probably goes back as far as the early Stone Age, over 300,000 years ago. During this period, our ancestors made a crucial intuitive leap that would forever set them apart from the lower species; they learned not only how to *use* tools, but how to *make* them as well. Using pieces of flint and stone to create simple hand axes, scrapers, and blades, our Stone Age ancestors could now equip themselves with the tools and weapons they needed to successfully confront their natural enemies, the wild animals.

Being successful hunters, however, required more than a working knowledge of tools and weapons and how to make them. Our primitive ancestors also needed to know where animals could be found. Where did they eat, sleep, and raise their young? Observant hunters soon realized that animals left imprints in wet mud and clay. By following these imprints, the hunters could more easily track the beasts to their water holes or lairs. These same hunters must have also noticed that muddy animal tracks actually hardened from prolonged exposure to the sun. Clearly, it would not be long before someone tried molding lumps of clay by hand and leaving them in the sun to harden.

With the success of this simple experiment, the craft of ceramics was born. Centuries passed, and experimentation with sun-dried clay continued. In the Neolithic Age, when our ancestors progressed from hunting and gathering to farming, the need was realized for stronger, more permanent dwellings that could be placed close to the crops. Using blocks of sun-dried clay as simple building bricks, these people proceeded to build shelters that proved quite effective in arid climates or during dry spells. A good rainstorm, however, easily destroyed these early homes by turning the bricks into mud.

A number of different civilizations, including the Egyptians, the Babylonians, the Sumerians, and the Romans, hit upon the idea of *firing* clay bricks—that is, using high temperatures to heat the clay, thereby giving it strength and permanently eliminating its pliability, even when thoroughly wetted. Some heated their bricks in specially built ovens called *kilns,* while others fired their blocks under burning mounds of straw or other fuels. The latter process took several days and often produced weak bricks that still deteriorated when penetrated by water. Only kiln firing, at temperatures over 1,000 degrees centigrade, was found to be truly effective.

Kilns were in use in the Middle East as early as four thousand years ago, but it was the Romans who produced the more sophisticated brick-and-tile kiln around the first century A.D. This kiln had two levels: the lower for the fires, and the upper for baking. The kiln, which was open at either end, was usually placed on a hill where strong breezes would continuously fan the flames. The ensuing high temperatures produced significantly higher quality bricks. The Romans would eventually carry this technique to France, Germany, Spain, and England, where the kilns were used to make strong, water-resistant roof tiles, drainpipes, floor coverings, basins, and storage vessels. With the fall of the Roman Empire, clay-firing technology fell into disuse and all but disappeared for hundreds of years. The Great London Fire of 1666 destroyed a city made almost entirely of wood; the new city that rose from the ashes was made completely of fired brick, ensuring that such a tragedy would never again occur.

Among the first industries established by the English colonists in America were brickyards. Salem, Massachusetts, was producing bricks over three hundred years ago, while a little farther to the south, communities along the Hudson River set up brickyards as well. These bricks were shaped by hand, fired, and then shipped to up-and-coming cities like New York, which provided a ready market for the bricks. More recently, the effects of World War II got many people interested again in ceramics as a craft and industry. As imports from abroad were curtailed, merchants were desperate for locally made items, and hundreds of backyard potteries became lucrative businesses almost overnight.

IMPROVEMENTS THROUGH TIME

As we have seen, our ancestors probably began using mud and clay to make simple and practical items like bricks and water jugs during the Neolithic Age. These were molded by hand and baked either in the sun or in campfires. The discovery of firing enabled early peoples to produce more or less permanent pots, jugs, and bowls that allowed for the more convenient storage and carrying of water and grains. It is interesting to note that many archaeologists believe human and animal skulls were used for these purposes before the discovery of clay firing.

Clay pots were probably made first, with deep, round bottoms that mimicked the shapes of skulls. Once fired, these vessels became stronger and practically waterproof. They effectively held precious seeds and water. But there was a serious flaw in their design: the vessels could not stand up on their own.

Craft skills improved rapidly, however. Round-bottomed pots were soon replaced by flat-bottomed vessels that did not tip over easily. Further refinements included the removal of stones and roots from the potter's clay, which meant structurally sounder vessels overall. The most important innovation in pottery for many centuries, however, would be the potter's wheel. This invention, thousands of years old, not only made it possible to shape a revolving lump of clay into a pleasingly symmetrical form, using the hands and fingers to guide the molding process; it also made it possible to manufacture great numbers of pots, bowls, cups—any object that would be hollow.

The potter's wheel, the introduction of different clay bodies and firing techniques to produce fine china and porcelain, the trend toward highly decorative vases and urns—inevitably, the craft of the potter soon developed into the art of ceramics. Today, thousands of years later, it is estimated that over 100,000 Americans express themselves artistically through clay modeling and ceramics. Many of these artistic ceramists remark that they are fortunate to experience the unique sense of personal satisfaction that comes both from working with their hands and from producing an object of lasting value from the very stuff our earth is made of: clay.

THE PROPERTIES OF CLAY

Almost all of the rocks found on the earth's crust contain the oxides alumina and silica. Oxides are compounds of oxygen and other elements; in the case of alumina and silica, these elements are aluminum and silicon. Often, alumina and silica occur in the form of a mineral called *feldspar.* Clay is formed when rocks containing feldspar disintegrate from constant exposure to wind, weather, or chemical action. When feldspar is exposed to carbon dioxide (CO_2) in air and water, it breaks down and yields alumina, silica, and other soluble substances that are easily washed away. The alumina and silica combine with water to form the clay mineral *kaolinite.*

There are two basic types of clay: *residual* (or primary) and *sedimentary* (or secondary). Residual clay is found among the rocks from which it was formed, often deep underground in deposits characterized by their thickness. Sedimentary clay is far more common than residual clay and is found in deposits by rivers, lakes, and other pools of water. While residual clay is purer than sedimentary, pure clay is rarely found. Eons of exposure to the elements have mixed clays with sand, salt, organic matter, rocks, and mineral oxides. These impurities give clay its wide range of colors. For example, if a large amount of red iron oxide is present, the clay will have a red or pink color; if small (or no) amounts of iron oxide are present, the clay will take its color from organic matter and appear black, brown, or gray. Absolutely pure clay is as white as snow.

Clay is found all over the earth, which explains why all civilizations have used it since the dawn of time. However, not all clays can be used for ceramics. Ceramic clay must have the following characteristics:

- Plastic (moldable)
- Porous (containing small holes to allow perspiration or absorption)
- Vitreous (capable of being hardened by heat)

Also, good ceramic clay should not warp, crack, or sag when fired. Since few natural clays meet all of these requirements, most clays used in ceramics are actually blends of different clay bodies.

FIRING

Why do ceramists fire clay? As we saw earlier, our primitive ancestors discovered that if clay was left to stand for a few days, the water in it eventually evaporated, leaving the clay harder than it was before, but also more brittle. They also learned that jugs or bowls made from dried-out clay were virtually useless, because once water was added to the dried-out clay, it became plastic again: the bowl or jug turned to muddy clay. Clay can be worked and reworked into innumerable forms and shapes that will become hard and brittle (or plastic with the addition of water) unless the clay is baked, or fired, in a very hot furnace called a kiln.

Once clay has been fired, its chemical composition changes. The clay becomes more dense, more durable, and more resistant to water penetration. Firing causes the clay mineral to decompose. Its water is driven off by steam; impurities change form or melt; and some of the clay's silica melts with impurities into a common mass that cools and becomes glasslike. This glassy bond is what prevents a fired brick from turning to mud if it is exposed to water. Ceramists call the process of hardening clay by exposure to heat *vitrification.*

CERAMICS: TYPES AND CHARACTER

Ceramics is a term with meanings as varied as its applications. There are many different types of ceramic products, among them pottery, whiteware (which includes china and porcelain), glass, and structural clay products (such as building bricks or tiles), which can withstand extremely high temperatures. Let's take a closer look at each.

Pottery is a generic term, referring not only to all fired objects made from clay, but to the shop in which ceramic objects are made as well. More specifically, the term *pottery* is used to describe porous articles that have been fired at a relatively low temperature. There are two basic types of pottery: soft and hard. Soft pottery, which is also known as nonvitreous ware, is unglazed, and can be easily scratched by a pointed piece of iron. If the same piece of iron has no effect on a piece of pottery, the pottery is labeled *hard.* Since the term *pottery* is so broad, it is necessary to put its numerous varieties of wares into three classifications: *earthenware, stoneware,* and *porcelain.*

Earthenware differs from other pottery primarily in color, which is usually a buff or a shade of white. A dictionary may define earthenware as "ware made of earth, clay, etc.," but to ceramists the word has a more restricted meaning; they use it to describe cream-colored or white porous bodies that are covered with a transparent glaze. Ancient Greek vases that were baked and glazed are an example of earthenware, as are common household crockery, brick and terra-cotta, and enameled ware. *Stoneware* contains a large percentage of silica in the clay which, when fired, causes the clay to become extremely hard; while *porcelain* is not only characterized by its hardness but its translucency as well.

China and porcelain are *whitewares,* a term that refers to the hard, white translucent ceramics treasured by so many. Although the words *china* and *porcelain* are used interchangeably in many countries, American ceramists distinguish between the two on the basis of use: all vitrified whiteware made for home use is china, while industrial whitewares are porcelain. While china and porcelain are both strong, white, nonporous, translucent materials, they do differ in body composition and are fired at different temperatures. Porcelain was first produced in China and was brought to Europe by Marco Polo in 1295. Europeans were immediately taken by the strength, color, and beauty of porcelain, and for years they tried to discover the Chinese secret of its production. It would not be until the beginning of the eighteenth century that a German alchemist and ceramist named Johann Friedrich Bottger (1682–1719) would succeed in making anything similar to Chinese porcelain in the Western world.

Structural clay products are the everyday ceramic items with which we are most familiar: roof tiles, building bricks, drain tile, sewer pipes, and stoneware. Stoneware is not as porous as earthenware and is usually less vitrified than china. This is because the intense heat used to fire stoneware tends to deform the heavier items. Weight and transportation costs of both raw and finished stoneware are two of the main reasons the items are usually manufactured close to their actual clay deposits. Potters in western Germany first produced stoneware jugs and vases in the twelfth century A.D. From the sixteenth to the mid-eighteenth century, much of western Europe's tableware was fine stoneware.

THE CERAMIC ARTIST

As an artistic medium, the appeal of clay has not waned, despite the fact that mass production has taken over so much of what individual artisans put their time and souls into. Ceramics has become a favorite hobby of people the world over for many reasons. Working with clay seems to stimulate creativity. Many people have remarked that they can express themselves through clay—vent frustrations, give free rein to the imagination. This is one reason, perhaps, why clay modeling has found a niche in establishments for the physically handicapped.

Ceramics is a craft with so much to recommend it. For the beginner, there are no particular tools to master and no special skills to develop before going to work. Age is not a factor: whether you are 8 years old or 80, you can still achieve the personal satisfaction of expressing yourself through taking basic materials from the earth and producing beautiful and useful objects. For the novice ceramist, machines are not needed; everything may be done by hand, and the necessary materials are easy to obtain. Schools and hobby shops often offer classes to those who would like to increase their knowledge of ceramic techniques and applications; and various organizations and publications offer information to the novice and experienced enthusiast alike.

If you are interested in taking up ceramics as a career, perhaps the best place to start your investigation into this fascinating field is your local public library. There you will find numerous books and articles that will introduce you to the craft, give you an appreciation for its history (and its more recent developments and applications), alert you to local and national ceramic organizations, and give you such vital information as modeling and glazing techniques.

WORKING WITH CERAMICS

Ceramics makes an ideal hobby for people who like to do things in their spare time. As we will see, many people have found their life's work by delving further into this fascinating field. Many others find working with clay fun and relaxing. But there are some basics to be learned. The following is a brief discussion of the process of making a piece of ceramic ware. It does not intend to tell you everything you need to know about ceramics, but it should give you a good idea of the basic skills and materials involved.

To make a ceramic piece, you first need clay. Clay can be bought from a pottery or hobby supply house, all ready for use. This clay will already have been crushed, washed free of any impurities, dried, and then mixed with proper amounts of sand and water to insure good working qualities. There are many different kinds of clay, which vary in color and feel. One particular kind to avoid is *plasticene,* which is not really clay but an oil-based material not suitable for firing. Clay sometimes comes in powder form, and must be mixed with water in order to make it plastic. Clay that has been mixed with water is known as *wet clay* and must be kept wet, or it will dry out. Wet clay is the type used to make pottery or any other articles that are to be fired.

The wet, plastic clay is shaped by hand or on a potter's wheel. The potter's wheel, as described earlier, is a basic tool used by a ceramist. As the wheel revolves, the ceramist uses her or his hands and fingers to form a round, symmetrical clay object. Performing this process correctly takes time and patience.

Once the object is completed, it is then permitted to dry slowly until all moisture has left it. The next step is kiln firing. For earthenware, the firing temperature is about 1,976 degrees Fahrenheit; for porcelain, the firing temperature is about 2,500 degrees Fahrenheit. The intense heat fuses the tiny clay particles, making the piece solid and brittle. To tell when the proper temperature has been reached, the potter uses small, triangular cones of clay that bend at specific temperatures. Several of these cones are placed in the kiln; when the potter looks through a peephole, it is possible to see which cones are bending, and thus tell when the firing must stop.

The kiln must then be permitted to cool very slowly, as a sudden drop in temperature would probably cause the pieces inside to crack or warp. When the pieces are cool enough to remove without gloves, it is safe to take them out. This is the first, or "biscuit," firing. The pieces are porous, hard, and brittle. A coating of glaze, applied by dipping, spraying, or brushing, will make the piece waterproof. When the glaze has dried, the piece is fired a second time; the glaze fills the outside pores and leaves a glossy coating on the finished piece.

FROM HOBBY TO CAREER: AN INTERVIEW WITH A CERAMIC ARTIST

Claire Youngblood was a 37-year-old homemaker with two school-aged children when she discovered ceramics. While vacationing with her family in the West, Claire became enamored with the ceramic pots, vases, and figurines sold by American Indians at roadside stands and souvenir shops. She watched intently as pots were "thrown" with seemingly effortless grace and skill. She decided then and there that upon returning home she would further investigate this fascinating field. "I had never worked with clay before—the art courses I had taken in college were strictly lecture—so I was really looking forward to getting my hands dirty!"

Her investigations led her first to a local hobby shop, where she learned that the YWCA held beginner's courses in ceramics at various times during the year. She also learned that most of the things she would need for her new hobby could be bought or ordered right at the hobby shop. "At the Y, we were taught different shaping and molding techniques, how to throw a pot on a potter's wheel, glazing, firing, the works. I found I had a knack for it, too. The others were asking me how to do things after a short while."

With her husband's help, she converted part of the family's basement into a studio and work area. "I put up shelves, and Dave put in a sink at one end and ran wiring in for the electric wheel and kiln." She began by making—and ruining—pots. "The beginner has to be prepared for a certain number of pots to warp and crack," she learned, "and for glazes to run." She estimates that most of her early attempts did not turn out right. "I think the most important things to remember are to dry pots slowly and to know what temperature the clay must be fired at. Learn to follow directions."

From pots and vases, Claire went on to work with cast figurines and sculptures of her own design. Experimenting with different glazes, she hit upon a mauve color that gave her work "an exciting dimension. I showed them to a friend who runs a gift shop, and she offered to buy the lot—right on the spot. I was in business!" Claire notes that as her interest in ceramics grew, and as demand for her work increased as well, she found herself putting out more money at first than she was taking in. "Dave and I discussed the finances, and it was Dave who made me see that to make money, you need money." She took out a small loan to buy some specialized equipment such as an electric grinder (to smooth the bottoms of pots after the second firing, when the glaze had been added), an electric spray (to glaze larger pieces), scales, molds, and rolling pins.

"I've become my own marketing agent, too. On Saturdays, I'll pack the back of the car with boxes full of statuettes, vases, and bowls that I sell at flea markets and craft fairs." She continues to sell smaller pieces through her friend's gift shop, and she now instructs at the YWCA. "It's a lot of work, but it's paying off," she says proudly. "I'm my own craftsperson, my own agent, my own bookkeeper—I'm the only person I have to answer to."

Would she recommend others taking up ceramics as a hobby or career?

"Wholeheartedly!"

CERAMIC USES IN INDUSTRY

The modern extensions of ceramic applications have served to divide the field into both a craft and an industry. While ceramic artists like Claire Youngblood mold and fire clays into shapes that please the eye and hand, industrial ceramists are producing a wide variety of products ranging from domestic tableware to electronic insulators to missiles and rocket nose cones. Because ceramic materials are fire resisting and can withstand extremely high temperatures, ceramic products have become part of a multi-billion dollar industry with major developments in the fields of electronics, nuclear power, and space research. It has been estimated that ceramic materials and products account for about 3 percent of the Gross National Product (GNP); but the industry's total contribution to the GNP may be as high as 20 percent, when other industries that rely heavily on ceramic technology are considered.

We have all seen ceramics at work in the arts, at home, and in the building industry. These areas account for only a fraction of ceramic use in the world today. Ceramic materials are now found in heat generators, insulators, microcircuits, appliances, and memory circuits. They play an important role, too, in the metals and nuclear industries. Because of the increasing importance of ceramics in industry and technology, many schools are now offering degrees in ceramic engineering and science. Career opportunities are growing for ceramists in such specialized industries as nuclear ceramics, electronic ceramics, and high-temperature engineering.

CERAMIC ENGINEERS

Ceramic engineers study the nature of clay and other earthy materials, especially when they are exposed to high temperatures to form new solids. They match known ceramics to new uses, and they develop both new ceramics and the machinery that manufactures them. Ceramic engineers are intensely involved in research, seeking new ceramics with special properties to meet the ever-increasing demands of modern technology and designing new production processes with lower costs.

In the United States, ceramic engineers work primarily in the stone, clay, and glass industries, although the applications of their discoveries touch many other industries as well. Job opportunities are plentiful; many industries require employees with expertise in ceramics, including heat-resistant materials, pottery, insulators, brick and tile, electric materials, metal coatings, glass, and abrasives. Ceramic engineers are even needed in the growing nuclear industry, as the fuel element of nuclear reactors and the structural components of the reactors are ceramic materials.

The student who wishes to become a ceramic engineer should have a strong background in mathematics, physics, and inorganic chemistry. Inorganic chemistry is the study of inorganic (nonliving) materials, their structures and properties, the ways they react to different temperatures and blends, and their resultant products and properties. The student should enjoy doing research and laboratory experimentation and be able to communicate clearly in both oral and written reports. Computer literacy is also a necessity.

Many industries hiring employees with an expertise in ceramics require a bachelor's degree at minimum. A higher degree may be needed by ceramic engineers who desire to teach at the college or graduate level or who want to do research. The job outlook is excellent, with openings in nuclear energy, defense, electronics, medical science, and energy handling. The following is a partial list of companies and corporations currently hiring ceramic engineers for research and development; the list has been culled from *Peterson's Guide to Engineering, Science, and Computer Jobs,* available at your local public library.

Private
Aluminum Company of America
Bell Telephone Laboratories
Champion Spark Plug Company
Delco Electronics (a division of General Motors)
General Electric
E. I. duPont de Nemours & Company
Hughes Aircraft
Lenox China, Inc.
Manville Corporation
Owens-Corning Fiberglass Corporation
Texas Instruments

U.S. Government
Army, Air Force, and Navy
Department of Commerce
NASA

SCIENTISTS AND ENGINEERS: UTILIZING AN ANCIENT TECHNOLOGY

Ceramic engineers and scientists play an important role in studying and applying the fundamental principles of bonding mechanisms—that is, the crystal structure of ceramic materials that accounts for their incredible strength and high-temperature properties. Matching known ceramics to new uses, developing new ceramics and the machinery to manufacture them, ceramic engineers and scientists are constantly engaged in research. An estimated 18,000 ceramic engineers were at work in the United States in 1990, mostly in the stone, clay, and glass industries. They seek new ceramics with special properties for industrial use and try to develop better, cheaper production processes for these ceramics. Many industries are demanding more and better materials; they are providing the impetus for many of the current developments in the ceramics field. The pressure to develop these materials is especially strong from the aerospace, electronics, nuclear, and communications industries.

In the aerospace field, the ceramist has been a key figure since the very first rocket launches. At takeoff and upon reentry, rockets are subject to tremendous heat, pressure, and friction. Industrial ceramists have designed the ceramic materials and coatings that protect a spacecraft from those dangerous temperatures and frictions. Once a rocket or satellite is in orbit, ceramic coatings reflect radiation that would otherwise heat the inside, damaging delicate electronic circuitry and possibly killing all on board.

Ceramic engineers have also designed the special glass windows of various spacecraft, windows that must be able to stand up to different types of radiation without discoloring. Since the same discoloration would occur on normal camera lenses in outer space, ceramic materials are used for these lenses as well.

Electronic equipment on satellites and in machines here on earth, too—must be insulated to withstand temperature changes and still function properly. Ceramic materials provide much of this necessary insulation. In fact, as the field of electronic technology has boomed in the past few decades, the ceramics industry has advanced right alongside, providing new techniques and materials that resist corrosion or oxidation or that have other special electrical properties.

Ceramic materials have been used as electrical insulators since the mid-nineteenth century. Stoneware and, later, porcelain were used for many years for telegraph or telephone insulators, fuse-holders, bulb sockets, and so on, because they were inexpensive to produce, easy to clean, and relatively easy to manufacture even in complicated shapes. Further experimentation proved that for high-voltage insulators, glass and porcelain were particularly suitable, as they could stand up to adverse conditions for long periods of time without showing signs of severe wear and tear.

Perhaps more than any other technical advancement, the discovery of X rays enabled ceramists to understand the crystal structure of clay and other earthy materials. With this newfound understanding of bonding mechanisms, ceramic engineers were able to develop vastly improved clay and sand-based materials, among them cements, refractories (nonmetallic ceramic materials, like bricks, characterized by their suitability for construction at high temperatures), and glass. X rays revealed to the ceramist the role that even extremely small amounts of impurities could play in changing the properties of certain ceramic materials. For this reason, many ceramic products are now produced in sterile environments.

Advances in ceramic technology have brought about new types of glasses that can withstand sudden variations in temperature, change color when exposed to light, or transmit light—or even transmit telephone messages! At this very moment, a fiber-optic cable no thicker than a garden hose is carrying thousands of telephone calls between the United States and Europe. Special ceramic techniques have so increased the strength of glass that unbreakable dinnerware is now being produced. One area in which ceramics has played an all-important role is the miniaturization of electronic circuitry. Working together, ceramists and physicists have learned how to produce very pure crystals of silicon, the basis of the transistor industry. In your own lifetime, you have probably seen the results of these advancements: ever smaller pocket calculators, computers and digital watches.

Ceramic technology is also evident in automobile emission-control systems, in power plants, in sewage systems, and in garbage disposal plants. All of these require strong ceramic materials to withstand extremely high temperatures and corrosive elements. In the production of nuclear power, ceramic fuel elements are playing an ever-increasing role. Industry estimates say that nearly 90 percent of all new nuclear electric power installations will use a ceramic material as the fuel element. Because of the high temperatures involved in nuclear reactors, many of the structural elements of nuclear reactors, right down to the control rods, are also made from ceramic materials.

Ceramic materials are also playing a part in the development of laser technology: different glass compositions are enabling scientists to extend the frequencies of the laser beam, which is now being used for everything from machining and drilling to delicate microsurgery. Piezoelectric materials, another ceramic product, are the active elements in sonar, ultrasonic devices, and phonograph cartridges. Magnetic ceramics, or ferrites, are used in small direct-current motors for automobiles, in computer memory cores, and in telecommunication systems. Cermets, a combination of metals and ceramics, are used in jet engines and brake shoe linings. Ceramic materials have been used as armor for helicopters and other aircraft, and in personnel armor, also.

In summary, the ceramic industry touches nearly every aspect of our lives and is a viable force in the nation's economy. The availability, adaptability, and durability of ceramic materials are just three reasons why the continued strong growth of the ceramic industry is predicted.

OTHER CAREERS IN CERAMICS

Because the field of ceramic science is relatively young, in many companies there is often no clear-cut separation for the job duties of people with advanced training in ceramics. The duties of ceramic engineers, which we have explored, may sometimes overlap with those of *ceramic technologists.* Technologists may have much the same background and interests as engineers, but technologists have also studied more advanced science courses including thermodynamics, thermochemistry, and crystal structure. Ceramic technologists will engage in research most of their careers, while ceramic engineers will divide their attention between research and production concerns.

Ceramic designers use their keen sense of color, shape, and proportion to design and decorate fine china and glassware. The ways in which clay can be embellished are boundless: it may be covered with a single glaze or decorated with drawings, incisions, and with many colors. The design and mode of decoration should conform to the shape and use of the object. To produce beautiful decorations, ceramic designers must have a flair for drawing, a knowledge of design, strong manual skills, and good taste.

Ceramic researchers are continually seeking improvements in ceramic products and production rates. Research is not the glamorous career television and movies have played it up to be; much time and painstaking care go into every experiment or trial. In this field, patience is truly a virtue. If you are easily put off by failure, a career in ceramic research might not be for you.

Ceramists may also go on to become professional engineers, salespeople, teachers, professional artists and sculptors, purchasing agents, and occupational therapists.

The field of ceramics is always growing. For those who enjoy working with their hands, and for those who thrive on research and experimentation, the challenges of a career in ceramics are many and exciting, as are the career opportunities.

WHAT TO DO NEXT

If the material in this chapter has whetted your appetite for more information about ceramics as a career, there are certain avenues that you will want to explore. Perhaps the best source of information concerning ceramics—its history, its applications, trends in the field, instruction manuals—will be in your local library. A number of excellent books will provide you with the information needed to decide if the field of ceramics is for you. Books on ceramics can be found for every level of age and interest; they will offer basic guidelines and information about this fascinating field. Don't forget, too, to visit your local hobby shop or ceramic shop, where knowledgeable enthusiasts will be happy to share their own insights and experiences.

More and more colleges are offering courses in ceramics for the beginner and the serious student as well. A cursory glance at a school's course manual will tell you if and when classes are being offered. Your local community centers, YMCA, and YWCA may also be teaching ceramic techniques.

Finally, additional information on the ceramics field and career opportunities can be obtained from the following:

The American Ceramic Society
757 Brooksedge Plaza Dr.
Westerville, OH 43081

CHAPTER 4

CAREERS IN CRAFT ANTIQUES AND COLLECTIBLES

Why include a chapter on antiques and collectibles in a book on craft careers? Quite simply, many of the crafts that are bought and sold in the United States and for that matter throughout the world today can be classified as either antiques or collectibles.

An *antique* is defined, according to the United States Customs Service, as an object that is at least one hundred years old. Some people have expanded this definition to include any object of value that is not currently in production. The definition of a collectible is similarly open to interpretation. For our purposes, a *collectible* is any object that is less than one hundred years old. In practical terms, the collectibles business is very much an American phenomenon. Although collectible objects have their origins in both the United States and foreign lands, Americans are far and away the principal buyers and collectors of twentieth-century pieces.

American interest in antiques and collectibles is a relatively recent development. It wasn't until the turn of the century that large numbers of people began to express a serious interest in collecting art and craft objects. Even so, up until World War II, most purchases were made by wealthy investors who were primarily interested in elegant objects from the 1700s and earlier. Following the war, a new generation of collectors entered the scene with more money to spend than ever before and an intense desire to own objects of the past that were made by hand. Their interest in antiques quickly expanded to include interest in collectibles—objects (such as quilts, furniture and pottery) of the early twentieth century.

Today, antiques and collectibles are a multibillion-dollar business. In the United States alone, millions of Americans have a passion for collecting, either as a hobby or as an investment. This interest translates into huge sums of money trading hands in the antiques and collectibles marketplace. And that money is spent on everything from furniture, rugs, and ceramics to glass, jewelry, and needlework. The list is practically endless.

Why is American interest in antiques and collectibles at such an all-time high? There are any number of theories to explain the boom. Certainly, as products of the machine age, Americans are drawn to works of the past that have the mark of an individual craftsperson and have been built to last for many, many years. Such works contrast greatly with the mass-produced goods of today that are purposely built to last for only a very limited amount of time (planned obsolescence). Many collectors also derive a great deal of pleasure from owning one-of-a-kind pieces. They feel that these objects are an expression of their individuality and even serve as status symbols. In addition, growing numbers of people view antiques and collectibles as an investment. Undoubtedly, the acquisition of the "right" pieces can be very profitable over time.

Craft antiques and collectibles include objects from every imaginable craft category. Some of the more popular include woodwork, especially furniture, pottery, glasswork, and jewelry. There are distinct trends and fads in the antiques and collectibles field. Today, for example, there is widespread appreciation for objects of the 1800s and early 1900s. Therefore, items such as handmade quilts, baskets, and hooked rugs are more popular than ever before.

Where can interested buyers purchase craft antiques and collectibles? They can visit antique shops, auction houses, antique shows, and craft galleries; or they can purchase crafts directly from their current owners. The size of antiques and collectibles sales operations and the quality of goods and services offered vary greatly from one establishment to the next. Therefore, buyers should be well informed about dealers and about the antiques and collectibles that they are interested in purchasing.

CAREER OPPORTUNITIES IN ANTIQUES AND COLLECTIBLES

The widespread interest in craft antiques and collectibles translates directly into a significant number of employment opportunities in the field. Dealers, appraisers, museum administrators, and restorers are in great demand, and they represent only a percentage of the career opportunities that exist.

The purpose of the remainder of this chapter is to introduce you to several exciting careers in the craft antiques and collectibles field. If you love old things and would like to work with them on a regular basis, read on and explore some of the most interesting and challenging opportunities in the field today.

THE ANTIQUES AND COLLECTIBLES DEALER

Today, crafts represent a large percentage of the goods that are sold in the antiques and collectibles marketplace. You need only browse through a handful of shops and shows to recognize that collectors are not only interested in fine art pieces; craft items such as furniture, baskets, textiles, pottery, and jewelry are often among the most popular items for sale.

Many collectors dream of turning their interest in the antiques field into a career as a professional dealer. Eventually some of these people actually do open antiques and collectibles shops of their own and suddenly find themselves in the role of "dealer." Others decide to sell their wares through antique shows, at flea markets, by mail, or right from their own homes. And a growing number of dealers use some combination of these outlets to give their merchandise as much exposure as possible.

If you are interested in starting your own shop, take some time to read through Chapter 7, *Starting Your Own Craft Business*. It discusses the potential advantages and disadvantages of operating your own business, the personal attributes needed for success, financial and marketing considerations, organizational considerations, and various other factors that you should be aware of.

If you decide that an antiques or collectibles business is for you, be sure to define exactly what kinds of merchandise you plan to carry. The majority of antique shops carry a broad assortment of goods and cater to a large customer base. The most serious dealers offer a narrow assortment of goods: they often limit their collection to objects from a particular time period, country, or material, such as wood or ceramics.

The most successful shop dealers have a detailed knowledge of their products, are up front and honest in their dealings with their customers, enjoy the sales function, and truly love antiques and collectibles.

There is no particular educational background that will ensure success. Many dealers are self-taught; they read as much as possible and continue to learn from their interactions with customers and other dealers. In terms of a more formal education, courses in art, history, and business are highly recommended.

If you are interested in selling craft antiques and collectibles but are wary of opening your own shop, there are other interesting and potentially lucrative alternatives. Antique shows, ranging from flea markets to highly sophisticated gatherings, are an additional sales outlet. Although many of the overhead expenses associated with operating your own shop are eliminated by selling through shows, there are some expenses like travel and show fees that should be evaluated when deciding whether or not to participate in a particular show. Dealers pay a rental fee for space in shows; many show dealers move from one show to the next since they are scheduled on a regular basis. You can find out about the times and locations of shows by reading the antiques section of most major newspapers or by reading relevant trade publications.

APPRAISER

The accurate appraisal of art and craft objects is one of the most important and fascinating aspects of the antiques and collectibles business. What functions do appraisers perform? Appraisers estimate the current value or worth of objects on the basis of specialized skill, knowledge, and a keen sense of quality.

Career opportunities for appraisers abound in direct proportion to the booming crafts market. In addition to the possibility of professional freelance appraisal, appraisers can find employment with the large number of museums, galleries, auction houses, and even antique shops that have sprung up around the country.

What qualifications are necessary in order to be a successful appraiser? Because of the dramatic growth in the antiques and collectibles market, professional appraisers must be specialists. They need to concentrate their study and efforts on one or two fields in order to remain knowledgeable and to make accurate appraisals of value. Specialized knowledge and skills can be honed over time by keeping abreast of any and all developments in one's field of interest, being well-read, and obtaining the necessary education and training.

In terms of education, although a college degree is not an absolute prerequisite for entry into the field, it can provide you with the background and skills that make you more marketable. More and more, a college degree is the key to the better positions in the appraisal field. Many appraisers come from an art history background that has been supplemented by more specific courses in ceramics, woodworking, jewelry, and other specialty areas. Graduate degrees in art history and related areas are also becoming more common among appraisers. Because of the international flavor of the antiques and collectibles market, the study of one or more foreign languages is highly recommended.

Aspiring appraisers should regularly visit museums, galleries, and auction houses, subscribe to all relevant trade publications, and continue to build a personal library of reference sources. Whenever possible, you should obtain experience working in a gallery, museum, antique shop, or auction house while pursuing your education.

Some of the larger auction houses and galleries offer internships or assistantships to top students. If you are fortunate enough to get one, you will be paid a nominal salary or receive college credit in exchange for your work. Internships are an excellent opportunity to learn the business, sharpen your appraisal skills, and meet other people in the same field of interest.

Financial opportunities as an appraiser vary widely. Those who work in auction houses or galleries can earn anywhere from $20,000 a year and upward. Appraisers' fees can range from $35 an hour to $100 an hour or more, depending on the estimated value of the work and the appraiser's reputation. For more information on this field, contact individual auction houses, galleries, museums, and the following organizations:

American Society of Appraisers
  P.O. Box 17265
  Washington, DC 20041

Appraisers Association of America
  541 Lexington Avenue
  New York, NY 10022

CONSERVATOR/RESTORER

Conservator/restorers are highly skilled specialists who are responsible for the care, restoration, and repair of historic and artistic works. As such, the preservation of valuable craft antiques and collectibles certainly falls under their domain.

There is no lack of work for adept conservators. Over time, many beautiful handcrafted objects fall victim to climate, poor care, and other stressful conditions. It is the conservator's job to restore such objects, if possible, to a better condition. In addition, the conservator is responsible for ensuring that objects that are displayed in museums and galleries are maintained under conditions that preserve the quality and integrity of the works. This can entail regulating heat, humidity, and lighting; determining methods of display; and overseeing the handling of objects.

It should be obvious that a conservator must be a combination of artist and scientist. In the restoration of art work, conservators must understand and adhere to the original artist's intent, while applying scientific principles to the process. Therefore, conservators combine detailed knowledge of art and art history with a background in chemistry and other scientific disciplines. This generally means that conservators are highly educated, often having advanced degrees in both an art and a science discipline. Several colleges even offer degrees in conservation science. This detailed education must then be combined with years of practical work experience in the care and restoration of a range of objects. Internships and apprenticeships are popular.

Conservators are employed by museums, galleries, and auction houses; some become freelancers and work for smaller museums and private collectors. Hourly fees for experienced conservators start at about $50. For more information on this field, contact the following:

American Historical Association
   400 A Street SE
   Washington, DC 20003

American Institute for Conservation of Historic and Artistic Works
   1400 16th St. N.W., Ste. 340
   Washington, D.C. 20036

MUSEUM CURATOR

Museums are institutions devoted to the procurement, care, study, and display of objects of lasting interest or value. Exhibits featuring handcrafted objects often dominate museum schedules. World famous museums such as the Metropolitan Museum of Art and the National Gallery of Art have carried some very notable crafts collections, as have the hundreds of smaller museums that can be found in virtually every corner of our country.

Museum curators are responsible for a museum's collection. More specifically, they may be involved in the search for, acquisition, assembly, cataloging, restoration, exhibition, maintenance, and storage of items of interest. Given all of these responsibilities, curators must often work closely with other experts such as conservators, researchers, and archivists to plan and prepare the form and content of an exhibit. Many curators also perform a variety of administrative and managerial duties, if they have a staff working for them.

What qualifications do successful curators possess? In addition to an appreciation for and detailed knowledge of arts and crafts, many curators have an advanced degree—often a Ph.D.—in some aspect of art history. A growing number have also taken some business courses. It is even possible to obtain an undergraduate or graduate degree in museum studies at a considerable number of colleges. The most competitive curatorial positions generally require a strong academic background supplemented by years of practical work experience.

Experience can be obtained while completing your formal education. Entry level positions on a curatorial staff can give you much needed exposure and lead to more challenging positions such as research assistant or even curator. Curators generally have five or more years of practical experience in a museum environment.

In order to remain current in the field, curators must continue to further their education throughout their careers by reading relevant publications, attending museum association meetings and workshops, and keeping abreast of new developments in museum operating techniques. For more information on a curatorial career, contact the following:

American Association of Museums
  1225 I. St. NW, Ste. 200
  Washington, DC 20005

CHAPTER 5

OTHER CRAFT FIELDS

There are literally hundreds of different types of crafts. Unfortunately, it is beyond the scope of this book—and in practical terms nearly impossible—to introduce you to each and every one. Chapters 2 and 3 profiled two of the most popular craft fields—woodworking and ceramics. The purpose of this chapter is to introduce you to several additional crafts, including some of the more contemporary ones.

If you feel that you are interested in a craft career but are still not sure of which craft to pursue, take some time to read through the information that follows. You will find brief descriptions of several craft fields and information on the kinds of background and skills that may be helpful in pursuing these crafts as full-time or part-time careers.

CANDLEMAKING

A candle is a solid mass of tallow or wax that contains a linen or cotton wick; the wick is burned to give off light. Candlemaking is a relatively simple and inexpensive craft whose roots date as far back as the fourth century B.C. Archaeological records indicate that even the ancient Egyptians burned primitive candles—weeds that were dipped in fat.

Although candles are no longer a necessity in our day-to-day lives, candlemaking is still an extremely popular and often fascinating craft. At shows and fairs around the country, it is not uncommon to see one or more candlemakers busily hand-dipping wicks in molten-blended waxes. They are performing for an audience that is drawn to the warmth and comfort of the candle's light. That same public buys candles of every imaginable color, shape, and size.

Candlemaking techniques range from the very simple to the very complex. *Dipping* is the oldest method of candlemaking and involves repeatedly immersing a weighted wick into a hot wax bath. After the dipping is completed, the finished candle is rolled on a flat surface to eliminate any bumps.

Although many candlemakers specialize in dipping, *molding* is certainly the most popular method of candlemaking. As the term molding implies, hot wax is poured into a container, or mold, that is heat resistant. As the wax cools, the candle is removed from the mold and may be buffed to create a beautiful shine. Individuals with an interest in candlemaking should be creative, have manual skills and good eyesight, and enjoy detail work. In order to make the transition from amateur to professional candlemakers participation in art and design courses and candlemaking workshops is strongly recommended. For more information on candlemaking, contact the following:

International Guild of Candle Artisans
  867 Browning Ave., S.
  Salem, OR 91302

JEWELRY MAKING

Jewelry pieces are objects of precious metal that are often set with gems and worn for personal enjoyment. Historical records indicate that jewelry was perhaps one of the first forms of adornment of the human body.

Jewelry makers design and create pieces of jewelry. Typically, this involves making sketches of designs for jewelry pieces and then constructing the designs in wax. Once a wax model is constructed, the next step is to pour plaster around the model, leaving a small passage to the wax. The plaster mold is then heated until the wax melts and runs out. Precious metals such as gold or silver are then poured into the mold. Once the metal has hardened, the jewelry maker finishes the piece. This may require filing, grinding, polishing, and setting gemstones.

Many jewelry makers work as apprentices after studying in technical or trade schools. Some pursue a degree in art, often with a focus on sculpture. In all cases, artistic ability and an eye for detail are crucial. Self-discipline is also an important attribute.

Jewelry makers can also specialize in setting stones, selling jewelry, and repairing pieces. When conducting further research into the jewelry field, also investigate goldsmiths, metalsmiths, and silversmiths. Be sure to talk with established jewelers, and, if possible, work in a jewelry store in order to learn all that you can about the jewelry business. For more information on this field, contact the following:

Gemological Institute of America
  1660 Stewart St.
  Santa Monica, CA 90404

BASKETRY

A basket is a receptacle made of woven cane, grass, wood, or other natural or synthetic material. There are an endless variety of basket designs. Basket shapes and sizes depend on function, materials, the kinds of *weaves* used, and the basket maker's creativity.

Basketry, the craft of weaving baskets, is one of the oldest crafts still practiced today. Although the exact origins of basketry are difficult to trace, archaeological records indicate that our prehistoric ancestors made baskets. It is also interesting to note that the Pueblo Indians of the southwestern part of the United States were called "The Basketmaker People" because of their superior basketmaking skills.

With the introduction of power-driven machinery in the late 1800s and early 1900s, basket making declined in importance. Baskets were no longer a necessity of life, and as a result much of the enthusiasm for basket making waned. Over the past two hundred years, however, basketry has experienced several revivals. Today it is highly regarded as both an art form and as a subject of great historical interest.

Basket makers should have a thorough knowledge of the range of natural and synthetic materials available to them and the specific characteristics of each material. Few tools are required to get started; a sharp knife and pliers are all that the beginner needs.

Individuals with an interest in basket making should be creative, have manual skills, enjoy detail work, be self-motivated, and enjoy the outdoors (the best source of basket material). Art and design courses and basketry classes are highly recommended.

LEATHERWORKING

Leather is animal skin that has been tanned; usually the animal hair is removed in the process. Because of its durability and flexibility, leather has been used for centuries to create both functional and decorative items. Shoes, clothing, bookbindings, furniture, and sculptures are just a few of the countless products that are often made of leather materials.

There are many different types, thicknesses, and grades of leather. For example, cowhide, the most widely used leather material, comes in many different types and thicknesses. The expert leathercrafter has a detailed knowledge of each of these characteristics and understands the implications of using one type of material versus another.

Leather can be carved, tooled, or shaped. The kinds of tools and other equipment that the leathercrafter needs to perform these functions depends to a large extent on what types of items will be created. Some of the more basic tools of the trade include instruments for marking and measuring the leather, scissors and knives for cutting the leather, and saddle stamps for creating imprints or designs in the leather.

In addition to having a detailed knowledge of the various kinds of animal skins, the leathercrafter should be creative and enjoy detail work. If possible, beginners should locate one or more established leathercrafters and observe their work. In addition, you should read books on leatherworking and take any relevant classes or workshops.

STAINED GLASS

Stained glass is glass that has been colored while it is being made. The origins of glassmaking are generally traced to the Middle East in approximately 300 B.C. The Greeks and Romans learned the art of glassmaking from their Middle Eastern neighbors. Over time, they developed techniques for adding color to glass, thus creating stained glass.

Historically, stained glass has been constructed into mosaics, or patterns, for church windows. Today stained glass is also used to create jewelry, window hangings, lampshades, frames, and a variety of other decorative and functional pieces.

Most craftspeople who work with stained glass purchase sheets of glass that have already been colored. Once a design has been determined, the glass is cut into shapes and then assembled. The pieces are usually held together with lead cane or copper foil.

The American public is very enthusiastic about stained glass products. In addition to the demand for designs created by the craftsperson, there is also considerable demand for stained glass workers who fill custom orders and who restore old stained glass.

Personal characteristics needed for success include creativity, a good eye for color, the ability to do fine detail work, and self-discipline. There are courses available in the art of stained glass. Apprenticeships with established stained glass makers are another possibility. For more information on this field, contact the following:

Stained Glass Association of America
    4050 Broadway, Ste. 219
    Kansas City, MO 64111

SCRIMSHAW ART

Scrimshaw is the craft, practice, or technique of engraving whalebone or ivory. Historical records indicate that scrimshaw art was produced as far back as the sixteenth century; today, it continues to be highly regarded as an art form.

The scrimshaw artist etches freehand illustrations—often whaling scenes or other nautical pictures—on ivory with the aid of various tools. Waterproof ink is then applied to the design, and it settles into the etched lines of the design. The excess ink is wiped away, and the ivory is then polished. Finished pieces are often made into jewelry or stand alone as decorative art.

Scrimshaw artists are often employed by jewelry stores and gift shops; many also work on a freelance basis. Personal characteristics needed for success include artistic ability and creativity, manual dexterity, aptitude for detail work, and self-discipline. Training should include art courses and scrimshaw courses, if available. An apprenticeship that provides on-the-job training is ideal. For more information on this field, contact the following:

Society of Illustrators
  128 East 63rd Street
  New York, NY 10021

National Association for the Cottage Industry
  P.O. Box 14850
  Chicago, IL 60614

BATIK

Batik is the ancient craft of hand-printing designs on fabric by using wax to coat the parts of the fabric that are not to be dyed. As seems to be the case with most crafts, the exact origins of batik are disputed. Some evidence suggests that more than 2,000 years ago batik garments were being designed and worn in the Middle East. Others claim that the roots of batik can be traced to Asia. Regardless of its origins, it is clear that batik as a true art form was practiced by the Indonesians in the thirteenth century. Their batik designs were highly sophisticated and symbolic of the Indonesian lifestyle and customs.

Today, batik artists use methods and tools very similar to their predecessors to produce clothing, wall hangings, and other decorative pieces of batik art. Fabric, wax, dyes, and brushes are the basic materials needed to get started. Cotton, silk, linen, and wool are among the most popular and workable fabrics. Wax (usually a mixture of paraffin and beeswax) is heated to between 300 and

350 degrees Fahrenheit; it is applied by brush or stamp onto the fabric. After the wax cools, the fabric is dipped in dye. The result is that the area of the fabric that is not waxed is dyed and the waxed portion is not. After the dyeing process is completed, the wax is removed from the fabric. Thus, a design is formed on the fabric. If a more complex design is desired, the waxing and dyeing process is continued through a succession of different colors.

The batik artist must be creative, have an eye for color and design, and enjoy working with fabrics. Many batik artists are self-taught or have received training from other batik specialists. In some instances, local colleges and craft organizations offer batik courses.

GLASSBLOWING

Glassblowing, also referred to as flameworking, is the craft of shaping a mass of glass that has been softened by heat. A glassblower is an individual who is skilled in the art of glassblowing.

Glassblowing is a craft that requires relatively simple equipment and is fairly easy to learn. Specifically, the glassblower heats a glass tube or rod in an air-gas or oxygen-air-gas flame and then molds the softened glass into the desired form by use of tools or by blowing air through a tube into the softened glass. This produces beautiful sculptures, vases, jewelry, and other novelty pieces.

The aspiring glassblower should be creative, have artistic ability and strong manual skills, and be self-motivated. Courses in art, design, glass, and glassblowing are highly recommended. In addition, an apprenticeship with an established glassblower is an excellent way to develop one's skills.

For more information on this field, contact the following:

Glass, Pottery, Plastics and Allied Workers
  International Union
  Box 607
  608 E. Baltimore Pike
  Media, PA 19063

American Scientific Glassblowers Society
  1507 Hagley Road
  Toledo, OH 43612

Glass Art Society
  P.O. Box 1364
  Corning, NY 14830

LAPIDARY

Lapidary, often referred to as gemcutting, is the craft of cutting, polishing, and engraving rocks, minerals, and gems. The term *lapidary* also refers to any individual who cuts, polishes, or engraves gems. Throughout history, humankind has regarded gems as extremely valuable and beautiful articles of trade and adornment. Archaeological records indicate that even our prehistoric ancestors worked with rocks and minerals of the earth to produce jewelry and other functional and decorative objects.

The equipment that the lapidary needs depends on what form the finished gem will take. Three basic forms are baroque, cabochon, and facet. *Baroque gems* are irregularly shaped stones that are tumbled or rotated in a tumbler machine for several days to create a smooth, shiny surface. *Cabochon gems* are produced by drawing an outline of the shape you want on a slab of stone and then cutting out the shape using a diamond saw. The cut-out gem is then ground, sanded, and polished. *Facet gems* are produced by highly skilled craftspeople who understand the optics (refraction and reflection) of gems and can operate very specialized gem faceting equipment. Faceted diamonds are undoubtedly the most widely known and demanded faceted gems.

The lapidary should be creative and artistic, enjoy working with stones, minerals, and gems, have excellent manual skills, and enjoy fine detail work. Courses in gemology and gemcutting are recommended. It is even possible to obtain a degree in the field. Art courses are also highly recommended. As always, an apprenticeship with an established lapidary is ideal. For more information on this field, contact the following:

Gemological Institute of America
   1660 Stewart St.
   Santa Monica, CA 90404

HANDWEAVING

Handweaving, in simplest terms, is the craft of interlacing thread, yarn, rope, or other fibers to form a texture, fabric, or design. Historical references to weaving date to prehistoric times; our ancestors probably used branches and grasses to produce primitive products. Further evidence of diverse yet fairly sophisticated methods of weaving have been traced to ancient cultures in various parts of the world; it is clear that the Egyptians, Greeks, Romans, and Chinese all wove cloth thousands of years ago.

Today handweaving continues to be an extremely popular and personally satisfying craft. The end products of weaving are as diverse and interesting as the methods and techniques of the craft. Practical products include everything from sheets to clothing; decorative products include tapestries, other wall hangings, and fiber sculptures.

The basic tool of the weaver is the loom, a frame or machine used to interlace at right angles two or more sets of thread or yarn. Looms are available in a wide range of sizes, styles, and levels of sophistication. The selection of a loom is a very important decision and should take into account the basic type of weaving that you plan to do, space availability, and your financial resources.

There are a seemingly endless variety of yarns (continuous strands of fiber) available to weavers; cotton, linen, ramie, wool, and silk are probably the most familiar. Learning how and when to use these various fibers is a process that requires time, practice, and patience.

The study of handweaving is a lifelong process; there are countless methods of weaving, types of yarn, and designs to be explored. Therefore, as an aspiring weaver, you should be prepared to spend many hours studying and practicing different techniques. There are many interesting books that offer valuable information on the field; in addition, weaving courses and workshops are growing in number. In fact, several colleges offer courses and even degrees in fiber arts. Established weavers are often willing to share their insights with newcomers to the field; therefore, apprenticeships should certainly be explored. For more information on this craft, contact the following:

Handweavers Guild of America
  120 Mountain Ave.
  Bloomfield, CT 06002

STITCHERY

The term *stitchery* refers to any work accomplished either by hand or by machine that involves the use of a needle, thread or yarn, and fabric. The field of stitchery encompasses such crafts as crocheting, embroidering, knitting, crewel, needlepoint, macrame, rugmaking, sewing, quilting, and tatting. Just a few of the end-products of these crafts include clothing, banners and wall hangings, soft sculptures, and murals; there are many, many more.

Most of us, at some point in our lives, are exposed to some form of stitchery; whether mending an article of clothing or trying our hand at some form of needlecraft, nearly all of us have had experience using a needle and thread. Sewing (the joining of one fabric to another with stitches) is the most utilitarian of the stitchery crafts and therefore is the one with which we are most familiar. This is because it is the primary method used in our society to produce, alter, and mend clothing. Embroidery (the process of forming decorative designs on fabric), on the other hand, is by its very nature more decorative than functional in scope. The end results of both of these crafts, however, are beautiful, creative products.

The various types of stitchery are popular hobbies for millions of Americans, and growing numbers of these hobbyists are successfully using their stitchery skills to produce hand and machine-stitched pieces for profit. Stitchery products are in great demand. Some of the more popular sales outlets for these products include craft shops, shows and fairs, boutiques, department stores, and other specialty stores.

The materials and tools needed to get started vary somewhat from one stitchery craft to the next. The basics for all of the crafts, however, are needles, scissors, and a fabric of choice.

For both the beginner and advanced needlecrafter, there are countless courses offered through high schools, community colleges, four-year colleges, and community organizations. In addition, there is a wide range of how-to books written on the various forms of stitchery. One of the best sources of stitchery information is other talented needleworkers who are willing to share their techniques and creative ideas.

Needleworkers should be creative, enjoy fine detail work, have patience, and be willing to put in long hours at their craft. For more information on stitchery crafts, contact the following:

American Sewing Guild
 P.O. Box 50976
 Indianapolis, IN 46250

Counted Thread Society of America
 1285 S. Jason St.
 Denver, CO 80223

Crochet Association International
 P.O. Box 131
 Dallas, GA 30132

Embroiderers' Guild of America
 335 W. Broadway, Ste. 100
 Louisville, KY 40202

National Quilting Association
 P.O. Box 393
 Ellicott City, MD 21043

CHAPTER 6

SPINOFF CAREERS

What additional career opportunities are available to craft professionals who would like to try their hand at other crafts-related endeavors? There are a variety of spinoff careers that you might want to consider. Some of the more traditional include teaching and demonstrating, writing, and starting your own craft business. Less traditional alternatives include craft photography and craft therapy.

As you read through this chapter, it should become evident that opportunities to branch out in the crafts field are limited only by your creativity, enthusiasm, and willingness to seek out new ventures. Hopefully, the information that follows will stimulate you to pursue all potential craft career alternatives.

TEACHING

Do you have a teaching background or an interest in teaching? If so, you should consider teaching crafts. Today, more than ever before, opportunities to teach crafts to others are flourishing. This is not surprising when you consider the overwhelming public interest in and demand for crafts.

Why do craftspeople turn to teaching? There are any number of reasons, but two of the most common appear to be 1) the desire to share one's love of a particular craft with others and 2) the financial rewards.

Many craftspeople report that they experience a sense of personal pride and satisfaction as a result of passing their skills on to others. Their love for their craft is so great that they want to share their feelings and skills with other interested people.

In addition, many craftspeople report that teaching can be very lucrative, either as a primary or supplementary source of income. Payment to craft instructors is generally made in one of two ways: in the form of a guaranteed salary or by the hour. Ten dollars and up per teaching hour is not uncommon. Some craft instructors make much more. In order to find out what the going rates are in your particular field, do some research. Talk to others who are currently teaching, and be sure to inquire into a variety of schools, shops, or organizations before committing yourself to a particular pay schedule.

What type of educational background is necessary in order to teach crafts? This is a difficult question to answer. In general, it can be said that the level of formal education required depends on the type of craft being taught and where the teaching is being done. For example, colleges generally require more formal education than craft shops. Many craft instructors are self-taught; they have little or no formal craft education. More and more often, however, craft educators have an associate's, bachelor's, or graduate degree in a crafts-related discipline and have also taken some relevant business courses.

In addition to an appropriate education, what other skills are necessary for a successful teaching career? Certainly, you should enjoy public speaking. If you are uncomfortable speaking before groups, practice. You can develop your speaking abilities if you have patience and determination.

If you are serious about teaching crafts, take some time to observe other instructors at work. You can get a lot of ideas about appropriate and inappropriate teaching techniques just from observing them as they interact with their audiences.

You will undoubtedly find that successful craft instructors are well prepared, often add some humor to their presentations, and make it a point to be as nontechnical as possible. They try to keep lectures fast paced so that their audiences don't get bored or discouraged, and they have a knack for generating interest and enthusiasm.

Virtually all craft instructors agree that a hands-on, laboratory approach to teaching crafts works well. This approach calls for introducing your craft, demonstrating how it is done, and then giving the students time to try a project themselves.

Craft instructors are needed in a variety of settings. Teaching and lecturing positions are available in school systems, including high schools, community colleges, adult education programs, four-year colleges, and graduate programs, with various community organizations, and in craft shops. Let's take a closer look at some of the more common markets for craft teachers.

Craft Shops

Craft shops hire instructors to demonstrate craft techniques to their customers. Students pay a fee to learn craft skills and, if necessary, to use the shop's equipment. Classes meet for one or several sessions, and the instructor is usually paid by the hour. Lectures are generally much shorter than they would be in a more formal setting, and the students spend more hands-on time producing their own handcrafted items.

Community Organizations

Many clubs and organizations are constantly on the lookout for new and interesting program ideas. Craft demonstrations are particularly popular with social organizations, study groups, community organizations like the YMCA and YWCA, and park and recreation departments.

Crafts that are easy to demonstrate, require few skills to learn, and are relatively inexpensive are the most favored. However, some groups are interested in in-depth craft instruction and have the facilities and money to offer more technical classes.

If you are interested in giving craft demonstrations to community organizations, you will probably have to search out opportunities. You can get the names of local organizations from area newspapers, mailing lists, and telephone directories. Contact them by phone or letter with a description of your background and the kind of program you would like to offer.

Private Classes

If you have the equipment and space, you can also offer private classes to individuals or small groups right in your own home or shop. The advantages of private classes are that you can provide more one-on-one instruction and you are able to work in familiar territory. If you set up your own home-based teaching business, there are also certain tax advantages to consider (some of these are discussed in Chapter 7).

Tourist Attractions

You have no doubt noticed craft demonstrators, like weavers and potters, at various tourist attractions, such as historic homes and amusement parks. There appears to be a growing demand for the services of skilled craft demonstrators at tourist attractions throughout the country. These attractions are always looking for skilled craftspeople who are willing to demonstrate their craft to visitors.

School Systems

School systems are a flourishing market for craft demonstrators. Many high schools and community colleges offer a variety of craft courses as part of their adult education programs. Instructors generally work part-time evening hours when adult students are available, and they are paid either a flat salary or hourly fee for their services.

In addition, more and more community colleges, four-year colleges, and graduate programs are offering craft courses and even crafts-related degrees (see Chapter 1). As a result, there is a growing opportunity to work full-time or part-time in one or more of these school systems.

The qualifications needed to teach crafts in each of these school systems vary quite a bit, but in general formal educational requirements are lowest in high schools and community colleges and highest in four-year colleges and graduate programs. Salaries follow accordingly.

A growing number of undergraduate and graduate schools are also offering business-related courses such as marketing, finance, and general business management as part of their crafts programs. If you have a strong business background, you can also investigate teaching business courses to craft students.

WRITING

Craft writers use the written word to inform, persuade, or entertain their readers. Opportunities for craft writers abound as growing numbers of magazine and book publishers take advantage of the extremely lucrative market for craft information.

From the craftsperson's point of view, writing about crafts serves a number of useful purposes. First, writing provides another outlet for the craftsperson's creativity. Second, having one's work published is an excellent form of publicity. Many craft writers have found that public interest in and demand for their craft work peak after they have gained exposure through their writings. Third, craft writing can be very profitable. Although few people successfully earn all of their living from craft writing, hundreds of craftspeople find it to be a lucrative means of supplementing their primary income. Finally, success as a craft writer often leads to other endeavors. For example, writers who have produced successful how-to craft articles often find a ready market for craft kits. Others have been asked to teach their craft and a whole second career has blossomed.

What skills are necessary in order to enjoy a successful career as a craft writer? Certainly, you should enjoy writing. But even more important, you must have the ability to express yourself on paper clearly and concisely. Many craftspeople often find it difficult to make the transition from producing and talking about their craft to explaining it in writing. Therefore, those who are able to take technical, often confusing, information and write it in language that is accurate and easy to understand do extremely well.

Before sitting down to write a craft book or article, make sure that you have something important to say. Then research whether or not other books or articles have already been written on the subject you have chosen. In general, the more original your idea, the better your chances will be of getting it published.

What kinds of craft information are publishers looking for? How-to books and articles are definitely popular. They should be written in a clear, detailed manner and should include illustrations (line art or photography). A second category of craft books or articles are those that are informational in scope. They may be a historical look at a given craft or offer biographical information on one or more prominent craftspeople. There are also directory-type craft books and articles that provide information on how to locate craft artists, craft supplies, craft schools, and galleries.

The numbers and types of craft books on the market continue to grow at a phenomenal rate. This is a sure sign that book publishers still consider craft books a marketable commodity. There are books written on every conceivable craft and on all aspects of the crafts field. The top-notch books sell very well and generate royalties (a share of the profits) for their authors over time.

Magazines that publish craft articles fall into two categories: general interest magazines and specialty magazines. General interest magazines such as *McCalls, Redbook,* and *Good Housekeeping* are always on the lookout for good craft articles. These magazines attract millions of readers and therefore demand the highest quality work. Although it is very difficult to get a craft article published in one of these magazines, those who do are paid well. The number of magazines specializing in crafts continues to grow. Although most of these magazines do not pay nearly as well as general interest magazines, *all* of their readers are crafts enthusiasts.

How should you go about getting published? Once you have an idea of what you would like to write about, study potential markets for your work. An excellent source of information about book and magazine publishers is the *Writer's Market,* an annual directory published by Writer's Digest Books of Cincinnati, Ohio. It contains brief profiles of most United States book and magazine publishers. The profiles include addresses, points of contact, phone numbers, royalty information, whether queries or complete submissions are allowed, and descriptions of the types of work sought.

Given the number of submissions that most publishers receive, the majority prefer to review a proposal for an article or book instead of the complete work. This is also advantageous to writers, who then don't waste too much of their time on a project if there is no apparent interest in the topic.

Once you have located potential publishers, contact them in writing. One of the most complete and upbeat guides to dealing with publishers is *How To Get Happily Published*, by Judith Applebaum and Nancy Evans (New York: New American Library, 1982). The book offers detailed procedures for submitting proposals and negotiating with prospective publishers.

ARTS AND CRAFTS THERAPY

You can also combine your interest in crafts with a professional therapy career. Art therapy is a very young but growing field that combines psychiatric treatment of patients with the use of arts and crafts as a therapeutic tool. There are still very few schools that offer art therapy degrees, but all indications are that the numbers will continue to grow.

CRAFT PHOTOGRAPHY

Craft photographers use their cameras and film to take pictures of craft items, craftspeople, and crafts-related places and events. Obviously, the craft photographer's most important tool is the camera. The professional photographer's camera generally is built to use a variety of lenses so that close-up, medium-range, or long-distance subject matter can be photographed. In addition, the photographer uses a variety of films and filters to take pictures under different lighting conditions. Some craft photographers develop and enlarge their own pictures; others send their film to photo laboratories for processing.

In addition to the skilled use of camera equipment, the craft photographer must be creative and have the ability to capture the personality of individuals, events, and crafts in pictures. Serious photographers must also keep up-to-date on equipment trends and attend courses and lectures to learn new skills and techniques.

What types of opportunities exist for craft photographers? A growing number of craftspeople are enlisting the aid of professional photographers to take pictures of their crafts. These pictures are then used in their portfolios. Craft writers also use professional photographers to take pictures to accompany their articles, and craft publications employ photographers to take pictures of a wide variety of subjects. It is also possible to freelance for newspapers and magazines; photographs of newsworthy craft events, places, people, and products are always needed.

Photographers are generally paid by the hour or by the project. Fees vary greatly, depending on your level of skill, experience, and the demand for your work.

RETAIL CRAFT SUPPLIES

Craft supplies, including equipment, tools, materials, and kits, are the lifeblood of the crafts industry. Without an adequate number of craft suppliers, craftspeople could not produce their wares.

Aware of the huge demand for supplies, a growing number of craftspeople with good business sense are venturing into the craft supplies business, and many have found it to be very lucrative.

Operating a craft supply store is very demanding. In order to be successful, you should have lots of energy, strong business skills, knowledge of different types and sources of craft supplies, strong people skills, and a willingness to take risks. For a more detailed look at how to go about starting your own craft supply business, refer to the next chapter.

CHAPTER 7

STARTING YOUR OWN CRAFT BUSINESS

Do you enjoy your independence? Does the idea of being your own boss appeal to you? If so, you should consider the possibility of starting your own craft business. This chapter will introduce you to the ins and outs of going into business for yourself and provide you with the kinds of information you need to decide whether or not you should enter the growing ranks of the self-employed.

If you are interested in using your craft and business skills to start your own business, you are far from alone. The entrepreneurial spirit of the American people is very evident in the crafts field. In fact, thousands of craftspeople have successfully made the transition from producing for fun to producing for profit. Once the transition from hobbyist to entrepreneur is made, the craftsperson becomes a member of the business community and immediately assumes the risks, challenges, and responsibilities associated with this new status.

Unfortunately, for every craftsperson who successfully operates a craft business, there are several others who have failed in similar attempts. Why? The management of a successful craft business demands much more than strong craft skills. As you will see, it also requires an initial investment of money, which can run into the thousands of dollars; strong business skills, including a background in marketing, management, and finance; knowledge of your customers; and the ability to sell.

There are several different types of craft businesses that you may want to consider. For example, you can open a craft shop and specialize in selling handcrafted goods that have been produced by yourself and by other artisans; or you can open a gift shop or boutique and sell a variety of goods, including handcrafted items; or you may want to start out on a much smaller scale and sell your crafts right out of your own home. Many craftspeople have also been successful with craft supply houses.

Whatever type of business you ultimately choose, be sure to do your homework before you make a serious commitment of time and money. With the right planning and business sense, you too can be a successful craft entrepreneur.

ADVANTAGES OF HAVING YOUR OWN
CRAFT BUSINESS

The advantages of working for yourself are many. First and foremost, you get to be your own boss. You do not have to answer to anyone but yourself and your customers. You can set your own hours and work at your own speed. You can chart your own future. If you want your business to stay small, it can. If you want to expand your operation, the sky can be the limit.

Second, if you work hard and your business is successful, you can make a very good living. Trends in the crafts field indicate that a well-run craft business can be very profitable. Talk to others who are self-employed in your field of interest to get a realistic idea of just how much money can be made.

Third, as a business owner or manager, you are able to maintain tight controls on the quality and quantity of handcrafted items that you sell. In addition, you determine how your goods will be displayed and what prices will be charged. In particular, you can sell your own work at full retail price and encourage the sale of your own pieces at every opportunity.

Fourth, you will have the opportunity to interact on a regular basis with others who share a love of crafts, including customers, suppliers, and other artisans. If you are the type of person who enjoys interacting with others, you will undoubtedly enjoy working for yourself.

POTENTIAL DISADVANTAGES OF HAVING YOUR OWN CRAFT BUSINESS

It is important to keep in mind that operating your own business requires a lot of hard work and a major commitment of your time. You should be able to devote a considerable amount of time and effort, often forty hours or more per week, toward making your business a success.

For many craftspeople, the thought of spending so much time on a business is both unappealing and unacceptable. Why? Selling and working on other aspects of the business necessarily cut into the craftsperson's "producing time." There just aren't enough hours in the day to manage the business well and to continue to produce crafts on a full-time basis. Eventually, some craft entrepreneurs have to make a hard choice: either stick with the business or return to their first love—producing crafts.

When considering whether or not to start your own business, ask yourself the following questions: How many hours per week can you realistically devote to the business? What other demands are placed on your time? (Family? Clubs? Church? Other interests?) How much time do you want to spend producing crafts? If you are honest with yourself when you answer these questions, you will go a long way toward determining if a craft business is really for you.

Another all-too-common reason why craft businesses fail is because owners find that they do not like the selling function. They would rather be creating than "pushing" their crafts. Unfortunately, many craftspeople do not find this out until it is too late and they have already committed considerable time and money to the business venture.

Therefore, before deciding to start your own business, be honest with yourself. Do you enjoy lots of interpersonal contact with customers and other craftspeople? Are you willing to expend the effort that it takes to make a sale? If the selling aspect of the business interests you, you will probably be successful.

Money (or the lack of it) is another potential pitfall. Many small business owners never even get their businesses off the ground because they fail to accurately estimate their expenses and projected income. Be sure that you understand all of the financial risks associated with starting a new business. Setting up a business requires money, often several thousand dollars or more. Many small business owners report that they do not break even on that initial outlay for a year or more. Therefore, before jumping into a new venture, take some time to seriously estimate your start-up costs and first-year expenses. If necessary, consult with a financial expert to work out all of the details.

One last note: as a self-employed business owner, you probably will not get paid vacations or some of the other benefits associated with more traditional jobs. Also, you will have to attract a regular base of customers or you won't get paid. If your marketing skills are weak, or if you become ill, or if your customers no longer need or want your services, your business probably will not survive.

It is possible, however, to surmount these potential difficulties with the proper attitude and know-how. If you are aware of your own interests and skills and take the time to research your potential business, you will be well on your way to being a success.

SOME IMPORTANT PERSONAL CONSIDERATIONS

Are you the entrepreneurial type? An entrepreneur is defined as a person who organizes, manages, and assumes the risks of a business or enterprise. In simple terms, an entrepreneur is anyone who establishes her or his own business. Following is a list of questions that you should seriously consider before deciding to become self-employed. Take some time to answer each one honestly, and then evaluate whether or not your answers are compatible with starting your own business.

1. *Personal Goals.* What are your long range goals for your own life? Would a craft business fit in with or interfere with your personal and family goals?
2. *Financial Goals.* How much money do you want to make? Do you want to be wealthy or are you content to live comfortably? What are your family's financial goals? Are you good at handling and managing money?
3. *Business Goals.* What are your business goals? Financial success? Personal satisfaction? Growing into a large organization or remaining small?

4. *Interests.* What are your primary career interests? Working with people? Working by yourself? Selling? Producing? Other?

5. *Working Preferences.* Do you prefer to work inside? Outdoors? In a hot climate? Cold climate? In the city? Suburbs? Other?

6. *Personality.* How do you rate yourself on each of the following: Friendliness? Optimism? Perseverance? Self-confidence? Sense of humor? Neatness? Dependability? Pride in your work? Readiness to smile? Willingness to listen? Speaking skills?

7. *Impressions.* How do you impress other people? Favorably? Unfavorably? Do you inspire confidence? Cause uneasiness?

8. *Qualifications.* What business experience, training, and other skills do you have which would prepare you to start your own craft business? Do you have any basic management experience or knowledge which will help you to get started? Do you have any special skills or talents that might be useful in operating your own business?

9. *Work Habits.* Are you disciplined enough to work long hours if needed? Are you willing to spend more than eight hours per day at your business? Are you committed to projects that you are involved with or do you give up easily? Are you a hard worker?

10. *Family Reaction.* Will your family support your decision to start your own craft business? Are they willing to make the necessary lifestyle adjustments (potentially less money and less time spent together)? Would a business disrupt any family plans? Would a homebased business cause any family difficulties?

If you are honest with yourself, your answers to these questions will go a long way toward helping you to determine if a craft business is for you. As you read through the rest of this chapter, keep these questions in mind, and be ready to take a harder look at each one.

CHARACTERISTICS OF SUCCESSFUL CRAFT ENTREPRENEURS

Although there are no specific educational requirements or personal characteristics that guarantee success in your own business, thriving craft entrepreneurs generally attribute their success to one or more of the following attributes:

People Skills. Successful craftspeople enjoy interacting with the public, and that sense of enjoyment is evident to anyone who deals with them. They have a cooperative, helpful attitude and truly believe that the customer comes first.

Artistic Talent. It is important to have an interest in and knowledge of crafts. When this background is combined with creativity and artistic talent of one's own, the possibility of success multiplies.

Business Skills. Craft entrepreneurs quickly realize the importance of a strong business background. There are several ways to get the necessary business training. You can take business courses at local colleges or universities; you can work for someone else for a while and get on-the-job experience; or you can be self-taught. Generally, some combination of these methods is thought to be the most useful.

Experience. Working for someone else for a period of time is an excellent way to learn the ins and outs, including potential pitfalls, of owning your own business. You have an opportunity to work with the public, see how finances are handled, and decide on a risk-free basis whether or not you should consider your own craft venture.

Knowledge of the Craft Marketplace. It is important to have a well-rounded background in crafts. You should be aware of the wide variety of crafts that the public is interested in and learn as much as possible about each field. You should also understand the craft marketplace. Who is your competition? Who will be your primary sources of supplies? What prices can you reasonably expect to charge? What have craft sales been like in your area?

FINANCIAL CONSIDERATIONS

Can you afford to go into business for yourself? Starting your own small business requires an initial investment of money. The amount that you will need depends on the type of business you decide to open and the size of that business. Initial expenses can include raw materials, supplies, equipment, tools, transportation, and rental property. You need to have enough money available to cover these initial costs and to keep yourself going for the first few months while you wait for sales to materialize.

The majority of new small businesses fail because the owners do not accurately plan for the first weeks and months of the business. They expect a positive cash flow from their operations right from the start, and in most cases that is an unrealistic assumption. You need to have the financial resources to get by for up to one full year while you wait for sales to take off.

Be sure to conduct a complete financial inventory before you start your business. First, review fully your own financial situation, and determine whether or not you have sufficient funds to get started. Then forecast your income and expenses using all of the information you have available to you. If necessary, hire a financial expert to help you evaluate your risks.

Time spent evaluating your financial situation will pay off in the long run and make the difference between success and failure.

MARKETING CONSIDERATIONS

It has been proven time and time again that successful businesses are those that meet a particular customer need or want. The crucial term in the formula is the customer. If you know and understand your potential customers, you will have a much better chance of offering craft products that they will purchase.

One of the most important questions that you can ask yourself is, "Who are my customers?" Ideally, you should be able to develop a detailed profile of your typical customer: age, sex, marital status, income, education, employment background, and interests. Once you have a good understanding of whom you are trying to sell your products to, you can focus your efforts on developing a product or products to satisfy that group.

Other important questions to consider: Is there a real need for your craft business? Are there enough interested customers in the area to support such a venture? Will there be a regular demand for your products? Can the people in your market area afford your prices? If not, would you be better off locating in another area? What is the competition like? Are there similar businesses in town? If so, what is different about your business, and how can you take advantage of those differences?

The bottom line is, why should a customer frequent your business instead of one of the others? If you have done your research well, the answer should be clear. Quality merchandise, fair prices, outstanding service, or some combination of these three will keep your customers coming back for more.

OTHER IMPORTANT CONSIDERATIONS

Type of Business Organization

Once you have decided to go into business for yourself, you have some very important decisions to make. One of the first legal questions you will have to consider is what form of business organization to choose. You have three basic choices: a single proprietorship, a partnership, or a corporation.

SINGLE PROPRIETORSHIP

This is the least complicated form of business organization. Any business that is owned by one person is called a single or sole proprietorship. The owners of such businesses often manage them; this is the case for many small retail stores and service organizations.

Few legal formalities are required to establish a single proprietorship. You can actually start one up today. Just give your business a name and you are ready to begin. There are state and local laws, however, governing the registration of your business, and you must file state and local income tax statements. All that the federal government requires is that you claim the business as part of your usual federal income tax filing.

The advantages of the sole proprietorship form of organization are that it is easy to start up and the owner is able to maintain tight control over all aspects of the business. There is one potential disadvantage that should be considered. For legal purposes, the business and the owner are not considered separate entities.

Therefore, if the business fails, the owner can be held personally responsible for all of the unpaid bills of the business.

PARTNERSHIP

In a partnership, two or more people voluntarily join forces to form a business. The partnership agreement can be either written or oral, but a written agreement is strongly recommended in order to reduce the possibility of misunderstandings. The services of an attorney to help put together the agreement are also recommended.

What types of information can be found in a partnership agreement? Generally, it provides for the division of profits or losses at the end of each year and makes provisions for the settlement of all affairs upon the withdrawal or death of a partner.

Partnerships, like sole proprietorships, are very easy to organize and offer some important tax advantages that you might want to investigate. For legal purposes, however, the partnership and its owners are still not considered separate entities; therefore, the partners can be held personally responsible for any unpaid bills if the business encounters difficulties.

CORPORATIONS

A corporation is a business incorporated under the laws of one of the fifty states. Its owners (or investors) are identified as stockholders. The extent of ownership in a corporation is shown by how many shares of stock an investor owns. Stock can be sold back and forth from one investor to another.

To form a corporation, you need to complete an application for a corporate charter with the appropriate state organization. Once your application for a charter has been approved, it is referred to as the articles of incorporation. The articles of incorporation explain the purpose of the new corporation, what types of businesses it may engage in, and how the company will be organized.

The next step is for the owners to elect a board of directors. They in turn appoint the officers of the corporation who serve as its day-to-day managers.

Most large businesses and a growing number of small ones are organized as corporations. The primary advantages include increased ease of gathering large amounts of money, the transferability of ownership shares, and limited liability of the owners. Limited liability means that the corporation is considered a legal entity separate from its owners. Therefore, owners cannot be held personally responsible if the business should encounter financial difficulties.

Which business form should you choose? There is no easy answer to this question. If you are serious about starting a profitable venture, you would be wise to hire an attorney or tax consultant or both to get as much legal advice as possible.

Accounting Systems

One of the smartest things a new business owner can do is take the time to properly set up the company's business records right from the start. Why is accurate recordkeeping so important? As a business owner, you will find that the financial information provided by your accounting system helps you to plan and control the activities of the business. In addition, financial information is often requested by outsiders, such as creditors, investors, the government, and even the public.

Some craftspeople understand bookkeeping and accounting principles well enough to do all of their own recordkeeping. However, if you are not skilled in this area, it would be wise to hire the services of a bookkeeper or accountant.

Employees

An employee is someone you hire to help operate your business. Many craft businesses are one- or two-person operations and do not employ extra help. However, the more successful a business becomes, the greater the possibility that employees will be needed.

As soon as you have employees working for you, you take on additional responsibilities. What are some of these responsibilities? Certainly, you must pay wages on time and keep up with the mounds of paperwork that are required by the government. You must be sure to fulfill your obligations regarding Social Security, Worker's Compensation, and Unemployment Insurance. In addition, you will probably collect withholding taxes and in turn pay them to the government.

Before welcoming a new employee to your business, be sure to investigate federal, state, and local labor regulations to be certain that you are meeting all requirements. You will find that there is a lot of additional paperwork associated with having employees, but the extra work is worthwhile if the bottom line result is increased output and increased profitability.

Business Location

Where should you locate your new business? This is an important decision because it will undoubtedly have some impact on how much business you attract. You should try to locate in an area that is convenient to shoppers, possibly in a shopping district, and close to major thoroughfares.

In order to make an informed decision, be sure to thoroughly research those areas that are of interest to you. Do local merchants appear to be doing well? Is there a steady flow of shoppers through the area? How much does good rental space cost? Can you afford it? Can you get the amount of space you really need? Does the town or city have any plans to make changes in the area that you are considering (that is, tear down buildings, add new roads, add new shopping centers)?

Many craftspeople who are just venturing out on their own decide to work right out of their homes. There are some distinct advantages to this arrangement. You can save on office expenses like rent, utilities, and taxes, and you may even be able to take a tax deduction for the space that you use in your home. And you can always fall back on your family for extra help when you need it.

There are some potentially negative aspects to operating a craft business from your home. This setup can put undue strain on other family members who must cope with the business twenty-four hours a day. To say the least, business calls and customer visits can become an annoying presence.

You alone can assess your individual circumstances and determine the location that suits your particular needs. Keep in mind, however, that the more you can separate your business from your personal life, the more rewarding all aspects of your life will probably be.

Other Expenses

When trying to determine your first-year expenses, be sure to look at all aspects of your business. What types of office supplies will you need: desks, chairs, cabinets, tables, computer equipment, pens, paper, staplers? What will you need in the way of craft supplies: materials, equipment, tools? Will you need additional insurance? Should you join any support organizations (like the American Craft Council)? Will you have to hire employees? Will you have printing and mailing expenses? Can you accurately estimate your monthly phone bill? Electric bill? What kinds of taxes will you have to pay?

It is practically impossible to estimate your expenses right down to the last penny. However, the closer you come to making an accurate guess, the better your chances of surviving and prospering in the long run.

CHAPTER 8

THE CRAFT MARKETPLACE

For the majority of aspiring craft professionals, two of the most important questions that need to be answered are these: What are the potential markets for my product? How can I tap into those markets?

If you are interested in selling your crafts to the public, this chapter is definitely for you. Its objectives are to introduce you to the wide range of craft markets that are available to craft professionals and to provide you with the kinds of information that will help you to decide if any of these markets meets your particular needs.

Certainly, it is beyond the scope of this book to offer a detailed profile of every potential craft market. Therefore, it is hoped that the information in this chapter will serve to increase your awareness of the ever-expanding variety of sales outlets for your crafts and stimulate you to pursue all potential sales leads.

CRAFT SHOW SALES

According to some of the most recent data available, craft shows and fairs are among the most lucrative markets for both full-time and part-time craftspeople. They can serve as a craftsperson's primary source of sales or can be a profitable addition to other established sales channels.

What are craft shows? Unfortunately, there is no simple answer to this question. In the broadest sense, craft shows, often referred to as fairs, festivals, or bazaars, are places where craftspeople come together to bring their work to the public. Shows can vary greatly, however, in a number of important ways.

Size. Some craft shows are huge operations that attract hundreds of participating craftspeople and thousands of attendees, while others are of the smaller, local fund-raiser variety. Size alone, however, does not necessarily determine the quality or success of a craft fair. Many large shows are notorious for offering only run-of-the-mill crafts, while some of the smaller shows offer an impressive variety of high quality, handcrafted goods.

Organization. Show organizers include craft associations and organizations, commercial promoters (whose numbers continue to grow), charitable organizations, and local civic groups. Organizers are responsible for providing certain services to participating craftspeople. These services generally include a space of the promised size, setup time, equipment if promised, and promotional activities to attract a sufficient crowd.

Location. Shows can be located indoors or outside. Popular locations include shopping malls, public streets, church auditoriums, exhibition halls, and open fields. From both the craftsperson's and customer's viewpoint, shows should be held in a convenient location, one that is close to major roads and easily accessible to large numbers of people.

Fees. There are two types of fees to consider: those charged to the craftsperson for participating in a show and admittance fees charged to the general public. In most instances, the fee charged to participating craftspeople for space rental and associated services is modest; it ranges from $5 to $75 on the average. Some of the more successful shows charge a higher price, and craftspeople generally agree that those higher prices are worth paying. Some shows also charge a commission on all individual sales, generally in the 10 to 15 percent range.

It is important to have a clear understanding of all of the services that are included in a fee before agreeing to participate in a show. In addition to space rental, the fee can cover the use of tables and chairs, help with setup, electrical outlets, security, show programs, and advertising.

Admission fees charged to the public should also be considered. A growing number of shows are charging admission fees that can range from $2 to $10 or more. The average admission fee is less than $5.

Show History. The prior history of a craft show should also be considered when deciding whether or not to participate. Questions to ask show organizers include: How old is the show? Has it been running for several years or is it brand new? What are past attendance figures? What are past sales figures?

Means of Entry. A craft show can be either open or juried. An open show is one that welcomes all craftspeople to participate, space permitting. A juried show, on the other hand, is one that prescreens or "juries" proposed entries. Generally, a panel of experts reviews each would-be participant's work and determines whether or not that individual will be invited to take part in the show. Some of the more typical categories used to judge a proposed entry include technical competence, mastery of the subject matter, and individuality.

Many professional craftspeople prefer juried shows because they usually attract the most successful craft artists and they enjoy a good reputation and following. Any well-run craft show, however, offers the craftsperson an opportunity to make money and to gain much-needed exposure.

Identifying Craft Fairs. How do you go about identifying craft shows in which to participate? Today, most of the major craft publications provide detailed listings of upcoming shows. Therefore, be sure to subscribe to craft journals that are related to your particular field of interest. In addition, the American Craft Council (A.C.C.) maintains a comprehensive listing of shows that are running throughout the country.

State arts councils are also excellent sources of craft show information. You can write to them and request information about shows that are being held in your particular locale. A complete listing of state arts councils can be found in Appendix D.

Festivals Sourcebook. (Paul Wasserman and Edmond L. Applebaum, eds., Detroit: Gale Research Co.) is another excellent reference guide to arts and craft shows and state fairs. Information on shows and fairs is organized by date, event name, and state. For each event listed, a contact name, phone number, and brief description of the event are given.

Finally, by maintaining professional relationships with other craftspeople, you will increase your chance of exposure to information about important upcoming craft show events.

POTENTIAL ADVANTAGES OF CRAFT SHOW
PARTICIPATION

Why should you consider participating in craft shows? There are numerous potential advantages cited by experienced show participants. According to a survey conducted by *Craftworker's Market,* craft shows were found to be the beginning craftsperson's best chance "for breaking into the field—for sales, exposure, a knowledge of public response to work and recognition through awards."

Sales. Craft shows can be a profitable retail outlet for your work. Statistics indicate that sales at craft shows are flourishing; as a result, more and more craftspeople are using shows as a regular selling channel, and they are meeting with success.

Exposure. Craft shows are an invaluable means of gaining wide exposure for your talents. The public is given an opportunity to evaluate your work, and you get an opportunity to expose your work to the public and to other talented artisans.

Recognition through Awards. A growing number of shows offer awards, including prize money. These awards give craftspeople much needed recognition, help to establish reputations, and serve as added incentive to produce high quality crafts.

Customer Feedback. At craft shows, the craftsperson has an opportunity to interact directly with potential customers. You can determine their likes and dislikes, test new ideas and designs, and examine reactions to various pricing levels. Most craftspeople consider such interaction with the public to be both personally gratifying and professionally beneficial.

Enjoyment. Many craftspeople report that craft shows are a lot of fun. Participation gives them the opportunity to be with people, share ideas and insights, make some money, and take a break from the day-to-day routine of producing their crafts.

POTENTIAL DISADVANTAGES OF CRAFT SHOW PARTICIPATION

Not all craftspeople consider craft shows a bargain. There are potential disadvantages that should be considered before deciding whether or not to participate in a particular show.

Time Constraints. Shows are very time consuming for craftspeople. Time spent traveling, setting up, and selling is all worth money to the artisan. If sales at a show are less than anticipated, the craftsperson is the loser in terms of dollars and cents.

Browsers vs. Shoppers. Many of the people who attend craft shows are there for a day of entertainment. They come to browse and to watch craftspeople at work, not necessarily to purchase crafts. Whenever possible, try to get information on a show's prior sales figures. These figures should give you a good indication of whether or not the public is there to spend money.

Remember, you are taking a gamble whenever you participate in a craft show. However, you can reduce the risk of failure significantly if you do your homework. Whenever possible, learn as much as you can about a show before deciding to participate in it, and be prepared to spend the time, money, and energy necessary to be successful. Good luck!

SELLING THROUGH RETAILERS

Many craftspeople prefer to have others sell their crafts for them so that they can spend more time producing their wares. Therefore, they turn to craft retailers. There are many different types of craft retailers. However, in general they fall into one of two categories: craft shops or galleries.

Craft Shops

Craft shops are retail outlets that specialize in selling handcrafted items. They can be found in virtually every town and city in the United States and are usually started by individuals with a special interest in crafts. In fact, many craft shop owners are craftspeople who have decided to go into business for themselves.

Craft shops provide a very important service for artisans. They perform the selling function, which relieves the craftsperson of a very time-consuming burden. The shops receive a fee for this service. How do they go about collecting this fee? Some shops buy craft items outright and mark up prices to cover their expenses. Others take craft items on a consignment basis. A commission is charged on all sales and generally ranges from 30 percent to 60 percent; the dealer pays the craftsperson only for what is sold and can return anything that is not sold.

One major advantage of selling through craft shops is that all transactions between the craftsperson and the storeowner can be completed, if necessary, entirely by mail. Therefore, the craftsperson who wants to sell on a larger scale is not limited to local markets. Potential sellers in far-off places can be contacted by sending slides or photographs of one's crafts through the mail. This method of contact gives show owners an opportunity to decide whether or not they want to see actual samples of a craftsperson's work.

Contacts with shop owners should always be made in a professional manner. Presentations should be as complete and polished as possible and should include a résumé that explains your craft background and experience.

A potential disadvantage of selling through craft shops is that profits on each sale will be less because of the expense of having someone else do your selling. Therefore, you may have to increase production in order to bring in the same amount of money that you were making when you were selling on your own. Only you can assess whether or not it is financially feasible to have someone else perform the selling function for you.

How can you learn about good craft shops? Start by contacting local stores. Visit the shops in person and be sure to provide them with a résumé and samples of your best works. You can locate shops outside of your immediate selling area by referring to crafts-related publications that circulate this kind of information. In addition, the American Craft Council maintains a detailed listing of shops and galleries that carry handcrafted items. *Craft Worker's Market* (listed in Appendix A) is another valuable source of information on craft shops located throughout the United States.

Craft Galleries

Although there are far fewer craft galleries than craft shops, galleries can be a potentially lucrative market for the craft professional. Many galleries exhibit only fine art, such as paintings or photographs. Growing numbers, however, are also carrying handcrafted items, often referred to as decorative art, as part of their collections. In general, these galleries carry one-of-a-kind handcrafted pieces of exceptionally high quality. These pieces are displayed as works of art and are often part of a particular show that runs for a given length of time.

Galleries usually take craft items on consignment and show them as part of an exhibit. The items remain on display until the end of the show and then, if sold, are dispersed to their new owners.

Some galleries operate as profit-making ventures, while others are primarily concerned with breaking even. The latter are often sponsored by wealthy craft enthusiasts, commonly referred to as *angels*.

Very few craftspeople have their work shown in galleries because the competition to be accepted is so keen and the number of galleries so small. Many craft galleries are located in large cities where the competition is especially strong. If you believe that your work is of gallery quality, however, be sure to make inquiries. Similar to your dealings with craft shops, the portfolio that you present to galleries is very important. Therefore, be sure that it is an accurate and positive reflection of your best craft works.

CRAFT TOWNS AND COMMUNITIES

Craft towns are places where groups of craftspeople settle to live and work at their particular crafts. Such towns are composed primarily of studios and shops dedicated to one or more crafts. The craftspeople share a total dedication to the pursuit of excellence in their given crafts. They also share marketing techniques and sometimes financial resources.

One of the most well-known and successful craft towns in the northeastern part of the United States is Sugarloaf, New York, a tiny hamlet of working craftspeople located about one hour outside of New York City. Because of its commitment to high quality crafts, the town as a whole has been very successful at attracting large numbers of visitors. Sugarloaf boasts more than 30 shops and galleries covering a broad range of crafts—jewelry, glass, ceramics, woodcarving, basketry, fabric art, quilting, leatherwork, pewterware, and much more. Anyone with creative talent and the money to rent space is welcome to settle in Sugarloaf.

The Pioneer Valley in Massachusetts is another example of a successful craft community. Much larger than a town, the valley runs from just south of Springfield, Massachusetts, to the borders of Vermont and New Hampshire. Well over 1,000 craftspeople live and work in the Pioneer Valley year round. They are supported by a large number of local shops and galleries that market their works to the public.

It takes a major commitment to one's craft to become part of a crafts-centered community and to live a crafts-centered lifestyle. However, a growing number of craft professionals are choosing this less traditional way of life because it offers a more focused, less pressured way to practice one's craft on a full-time basis.

MAIL ORDER SALES

The popularity of mail order as a method of selling handcrafted goods is at an all-time high. Think about it: The United States Postal Service gives businesspeople access to literally millions of potential customers. Studies indicate that those potential customers are buying more products by mail—including crafts—than ever before. As a result, many craft professionals consider mail order sales the mainstay of their business, while many, many more use it as a profitable addition to other established marketing channels.

What is mail order selling? Mail order involves contacting prospective customers by mail in one of two ways. *Direct mail advertising* entails contacting potential customers by mail on a one-on-one basis. In general, this means sending a brochure, price list, catalog, or other printed advertisement directly to the customer. The seller can obtain a list of names and addresses of prospective mail order customers from any one of a number of sources. Past customers are certainly a valuable list. It is also possible to purchase lists of names and addresses from mailing list houses—companies that put together and sell lists to others.

The second method of mail order selling is by means of *advertisements in publications,* such as crafts-related magazines. Magazine advertising, like direct mail advertising, can be quite costly, but it can also be quite profitable. If you look through the back pages of most craft publications, you will see countless advertisements for finished crafts, craft kits, and craft supplies. These same ads show up month after month because they have been found to be a profitable means of selling craft items.

It is important to understand that mail order selling is not as easy as it often appears to be. In fact, the mail order business is highly complex and extremely competitive. First, you need a considerable amount of capital for expenses such as printing, postage, mailing lists, and advertising space, Second, you need to have a thorough understanding of your markets in order to be sure that you are reaching them. This requires research and some degree of luck. Third, mail order selling does not produce instant profits. Many months can pass before you see any money from your efforts.

Why do people shop by mail? For the most part, people purchase items by mail that they cannot go out and buy locally. Therefore, if you have a product that is different and hard to come by, it may sell well by mail. On the other hand, if you produce crafts that can easily be purchased in local craft shops, you probably will not be very successful with mail order sales. Research indicates that the most profitable crafts-related mail order items have been do-it-yourself kits and hard-to-find craft supplies.

Before deciding to sell your product through the mail, be sure to study your market thoroughly and determine whether or not your product is a good mail order candidate. Then have patience. If you have a good product, in time the sales will come.

COOPERATIVE VENTURES

A craft cooperative is a business formed by a group of people to obtain certain services for themselves more effectively and more economically than they could obtain those same services individually. Most craft cooperatives are operated on a nonprofit basis. Participants generally pay a minimal fee to be a member of the cooperative.

What are the advantages of joining a cooperative venture? Most cooperatives are formed because members have a need for central marketing services, something they are unable to provide on their own. Some craft cooperatives employ marketing staff specialists; their primary responsibility is to oversee all marketing functions such as sales, advertising, and purchasing.

In addition, cooperatives often purchase craft supplies at wholesale prices, offer group insurance, have technical assistance programs, and provide various other useful services. In exchange for these services, cooperative members agree to share information about craft sales outlets and suppliers and keep one another informed about potential buyers.

Some craft stores are run as cooperatives. Members agree to help run the store for specified periods of time in exchange for the right to sell their own items in the store.

Before joining a cooperative, it is recommended that you take some time to talk to individuals who are co-op members and gather as much information as you can on the subject.

OTHER POTENTIAL SALES OUTLETS

Companies and Manufacturers. Companies and manufacturers can be a very lucrative market for craft items. For example, some companies buy the rights to do-it-yourself kits, such as needlepoint, macrame, and decoupage, which they in turn reproduce and sell to the public. Other companies buy the rights to craft designs or "prototypes" for reproduction on a much larger scale.

There is a business market for all types of crafts, from, woodworking and ceramics to metalworking and leathercrafts. If you believe that your craft piece has market potential, make a conscientious effort to investigate all potential buyers. The best way to make initial contact with prospective companies and manufacturers is by mail; be sure to include samples or slides of your best craft work.

Colleges and Universities. More and more colleges and universities are offering marketing opportunities for craftworkers. Craft exhibits are commonplace on college campuses and offer craftspeople an opportunity to gain exposure in the college community. Sales of craft items are also common. College bookstores sell craft items; some student organizations sponsor craft professionals for a percentage of sales; and craft shows, fairs, and galleries are often student-run.

It is important to keep in mind that, given the expenses of the average college student, the prices of crafts sold in college communities must be reasonable. Sales of crafts in the $20 to $50 range have been most successful. If you are interested in craft-marketing activities at local colleges and universities, contact the Director of Student Activities at each school.

Architectural and Interior Design Firms. Without a doubt, there are extremely lucrative craft markets in the architectural and interior design fields. Businesses in these fields are constantly on the lookout for talented craft professionals. If you are successful, your work may find its way into a newly decorated home or business, and that may be the beginning of a long-term relationship with a design firm.

Restaurants, Hotels, Banks, Department Stores, Business Offices. All of these businesses need to decorate to attract customers. For example, the offices of doctors, lawyers, dentists, bankers, and other business executives often need the creative touch of a craft professional. Talk to management to see if it is possible to exhibit your crafts. The displays will undoubtedly create interest and possibly sales.

Publishers. Publishers, especially those of craft-related periodicals and books, are always on the lookout for good craft articles and illustrations. For a more detailed look at this opportunity, refer to Chapter 6.

CHAPTER 9

WHAT TO DO NEXT

Many people approach career planning haphazardly, and, as a result, are dissatisfied with their work. This is unfortunate, especially when you consider the many hours that most of us spend at our jobs each day. You can avoid being another casualty of poor career planning by taking the time to determine your craft career goals and to map out a strategy for attaining them. By doing so, you will be ensuring yourself a satisfying and rewarding future in the craft marketplace.

This chapter offers some basic guidelines for engaging in craft career planning and job hunting. If you desire additional information or assistance, you should consult your local library. A number of excellent reference sources provide step-by-step career guidance. For example, *What Color is Your Parachute?*, by Richard Nelson Bolles, is a widely acclaimed career-planning guide, and there are many others.

DETERMINING YOUR CAREER GOALS

Before you commit yourself to a particular craft career, it is important that you clarify your personal career goals. Your goals should be based on a clear understanding of your individual characteristics and background and how they match up with the career that is of interest to you. Once you have such an understanding, you will find it much easier to find a satisfying position in the crafts field.

CONDUCTING A PERSONAL INVENTORY

To get a better understanding of the types of work you may be qualified for and enjoy, you should conduct a complete analysis of your interests, abilities, skills, and past accomplishments. Some of the questions you may want to consider include the following:

- What types of work do you really enjoy doing? What types of work do you dislike? For example, do you enjoy detail work, lots of people interaction, problem solving, writing, working with your hands? Be specific.
- Do you have any special skills or abilities that you enjoy using? For example, are you skilled at doing slow, careful work that requires attention to detail and manual dexterity?
- Do you enjoy working closely with other people, or do you prefer to work by yourself?
- Are you looking for a long-term career opportunity? Are you interested in growth potential?
- Do you enjoy responsibility? Are you looking for a position with responsibility?
- How well do you handle pressure? Do you want a position that has a lot of pressure associated with it?
- What aspects of past jobs did you like or dislike?
- How do you rate your communications skills? Do you enjoy writing or public speaking?
- What is your educational background?

By studying your answers to questions such as these, you should begin to develop a better understanding of the kinds of work you probably should and should not consider. For example, a position as a woodworker is probably not for you if you do not especially enjoy working with your hands and do not like being confined to one area for long periods of time. On the other hand, if you like people, have an outgoing personality, and have strong communication skills, you should possibly consider opening up your own craft shop.

EXPLORING CAREER OPTIONS IN THE CRAFTS FIELD

After conducting a personal inventory, you should explore career options in the craft field that interests you. As an aspiring craft professional, you will want to investigate all potential job options in your field of interest. Your research should result in a list of various types of employment options, the responsibilities associated with each, skill requirements, educational requirements, working conditions, salary ranges, and opportunities for growth and advancement.

This information can be gathered from a number of different sources. There are several excellent craft reference sources available. Appendix A provides a listing of some of those reference materials. You should also spend some time talking to people already employed in the craft field that interests you. Informational interviews with craft professionals can give you a much better idea of what specific jobs are really like. Finally, you may want to get in touch with professional associations, such as those listed at various points throughout this book and in Appendix C. These organizations can provide you with career information and may even have information about possible career opportunities in your locality.

ESTABLISHING YOUR PERSONAL CAREER GOALS

Once you have taken a personal inventory and have explored possible career options, it is time to establish your personal career goals. Specifically, the kinds of questions you will want to answer include the following:

- What types of craft positions are of interest to you?
- Do you have the necessary personal traits and technical skills for those positions?
- Are you willing to return to school to develop or upgrade your skills?
- What salary do you require?
- What benefits do you expect?
- In what locality do you want to find employment?
- Do you want to work for a specific company or organization, or do you plan to be self-employed?
- Are you looking for full-time or part-time work?
- What hours can you work?
- Are you interested in responsibility and growth potential?

The result of this process should be a clearly stated career goal. For example, your immediate goal might be to obtain a permanent, full-time position as an entry-level museum curatorial assistant, making at least $20,400 per year, working for a museum in the New York metropolitan area. Your long-term goal might be to attain the position of curator in that or a similar museum within a five-year period.

BECOMING QUALIFIED

Once you have clearly outlined your craft career goals, you need to develop a strategy for achieving those goals. If you already have the educational background and skills required for the position that interests you, you can start investigating potential employment possibilities. However, if you are not yet qualified, you will need to take steps to remedy the situation.

Ask yourself the following questions: What are the minimum educational requirements and skills necessary for the kind of work that I am interested in? How can I meet those requirements? If you have the time and money, you should seriously consider returning to a classroom environment to obtain the necessary training. If you cannot afford full-time training, it is still possible to acquire crafts-related skills on a part-time basis. Investigate the evening programs at local colleges and look into the kinds of courses that are offered by organizations such as the YMCA and YWCA. In addition, talk with local craft professionals in your field of interest about the possibility of an apprenticeship. If necessary, volunteer some of your time in exchange for exposure to the information and skills that you need. The point is to try to get as much hands-on work experience as you can, paid or volunteer. Experience will sharpen your skills and will make you much more marketable when you enter the craft job market.

INVESTIGATING PROSPECTIVE EMPLOYERS

Because they are anxious to put their newly acquired skills to work, many people take the first job that they find out about or are offered. Do not fall into this trap. Keep in mind that finding the right opportunity will probably involve considerable time and research. Therefore, do not be easily discouraged; your commitment of time and energy will undoubtedly pay off in a rewarding career in the crafts field.

Where should you look for prospective opportunities? The following list represents some of the more common sources of craft career information. If possible, explore them all. In addition, be creative, use your imagination, and the right position will eventually materialize.

Your Present Employer. Do you enjoy working for your present organization? If so, investigate crafts-related employment opportunities right in your present work situation. If opportunities do exist, make sure that you let the right people know that you are interested and want to be considered. In addition, discuss opportunities for growth and advancement. There may be no need for you to extend your job search any further than your present place of employment.

School Placement Offices. Some employers list available job openings with school placement offices. They do so because of the excellent reputations associated with the graduates of particular schools. If you are currently enrolled at a school that offers crafts-related training and they have a placement office, be sure to take advantage of this excellent job information source.

Help-Wanted Advertisements. One of the easiest ways to find out about opportunities in your community is to read the daily and Sunday classified sections of the local newspaper. From time to time, opportunities in crafts-related endeavors are listed through them. The ads can be a valuable source of information about which organizations are hiring, what positions are available, the nature of particular jobs, types of skills in demand, experience requirements, and salary levels.

Help-wanted ads also often appear in magazines and newspapers associated with particular crafts. If, for example, you are interested in a position in the ceramics field, you should take a look at ceramics trade journals.

Employment Services. The main goal of employment agencies and temporary help services is to match employers with employees. Employment agencies fill permanent positions while temporary services fill temporary job openings. Both types of employment services fill crafts-related positions for employers and should not be overlooked as a job source. If you do become involved with an employment service, make sure that you understand any fee arrangements before you sign a contract.

Your Public Library. Your local public library can provide a wealth of information about prospective employment opportunities in your community and throughout the country. Business and other directories offer detailed information about a wide variety of organizations and industries. Most libraries can also provide you with lists of business and professional organizations, trade associations, and community organizations that are relevant to your field of interest. The reference librarian can assist you in gathering this information.

Government Employment Offices. Federal, state, and local government organizations employ personnel in craft-related positions. Government employment offices or job information centers maintain lists of all currently available positions and the specific requirements for those positions. In most instances, there are standard procedures for applying for these jobs and deadlines for filing applications. You can obtain this information directly from the employment offices.

Word of Mouth. Use of personal contacts has been found to be one of the most effective ways of finding out about job openings and getting a foot in the door—especially in the crafts field. Therefore, you should let as many people as possible know that you are looking for a job and what your interests are. This means family, friends, former employers, and anyone else who may have information about job openings in your particular field of interest. Specifically, be sure to talk to other craft professionals who are currently employed. They often have access to information on employment opportunities that is not readily available to those outside of the "network."

The Phone Book. Your phone book can serve as a business directory. If you are interested in working for a particular type of shop or organization, it makes sense to look in the yellow pages of your phone book for a listing of all craft organizations in your area in that line of work.

Gathering details about prospective employers is no easy task. If possible, the information that you amass about each one should include the following: a company profile, types of positions available, position descriptions, necessary qualifications, salaries and other benefits, opportunities for advancement, and working conditions. With all of this information at your fingertips, you can then make an intelligent decision about those individual opportunities that you are interested in pursuing.

PREPARING A RÉSUMÉ AND COVER LETTER

In many cases, your first contact with a prospective employer will be by mail. It is important, therefore, that you prepare a cover letter and résumé that will make a favorable first impression and get you an interview.

The cover letter that accompanies your résumé serves a number of important functions. It briefly introduces you to the prospective employer; it expresses your interest in a particular position; it mentions your qualifications for the job; and it explains why you want to work for that particular organization. Your cover letter should be brief but interesting and informative and, like your résumé, should be meticulously typewritten.

The résumé itself should be an accurate, interesting, and attractive presentation of your background, skills, and abilities. There are many different theories as to how a résumé should be organized and the types of information it should include. Certainly, you will want to put your name, address, and phone number at the very top. For a specific position in the crafts field, you will need to list all relevant education and training. And of course, you will need to point out all relevant work experience—paid or volunteer. You may also want to include type of work sought, honors and offices, memberships in professional associations, and references. Most résumés end with a statement like: "References available upon request."

If you are just entering the craft job market, you will want to stress your relevant training and educational background. If you are already employed in the crafts field, emphasize *both* your experience and training.

The way that all this information is organized is largely a matter of personal taste and preference. There are two basic résumé styles. The chronological résumé lists your work experience in chronological order, beginning with your most recent job. The functional résumé expresses your qualifications in categories, such as sales and management skills. It emphasizes job functions instead of dates of employment. Numerous books have been written on the résumé writing process, and you should refer to several of them before making a final determination.

In some instances, you will have to go directly to an organization's employment office and fill out one of their standard applications before being considered for a position. If this is the case, be sure to bring all relevant information with you, including names and phone numbers of references and any other important names and dates. When filling out the application, be neat and thorough. Like your résumé, it is a reflection of you.

INTERVIEWING

The job interview is the next step in the job-hunting process. This is often the step that terrifies interviewees and can make or break the job offer. The best way to overcome your fears is to be prepared for the interview and to keep in mind that you have a skill that is needed by the interviewer's organization.

Before you go to the interview, find out as much as possible about your prospective employer and the job you are applying for. Make a list of any questions you may have. If you do not know the salary being offered for the position, have a particular salary range in mind. Review your background and qualifications, and be prepared to discuss them in detail. In addition, do the following:

- Dress appropriately. For most interviews in a formal work setting, a suit for a man and a dress for a woman are appropriate.
- Show interest and enthusiasm for the job and the organization. A good attitude is often as important as your actual qualifications.
- Prepare ahead of time for difficult questions. These might include the following: Tell me about yourself? Where do you want to be five or ten years from now? What are your major strengths or weaknesses? What special contribution can you make to our organization? What kind of salary are you looking for? Why are you interested in this particular position? How long do you plan to work for our organization?

Many career planning books offer valuable advice about the interviewing process, including how to handle such tough questions. You would be wise to spend some time reading and preparing for the job interview. It will be time well spent.

FOLLOWING UP THE INTERVIEW

After every interview, be sure to thank the interviewer for her or his time, and remember to send a follow-up thank-you letter. A short note of thanks often makes a lasting and favorable impression and provides you with one more chance to express your interest in the job.

CHOOSING THE RIGHT JOB

Hopefully, the result of all of this hard work will be one or several job offers from organizations that are of interest to you. In the final analysis, only you can decide which job offer is the right one. Before you make a decision, be sure to review all of the facts about each position, and review your personal goals. If you are lucky, the choice will be clear.

CONTINUING TO PLAN YOUR CAREER

The fact that you are reading this book indicates your interest in planning for your future. It is important to keep in mind that career planning does not end once you find suitable employment. Indeed, it is a process that should continue throughout your professional life.

As a craft professional, there are a number of things that you should continue to do throughout your career. Read, take additional courses, attend workshops and seminars, join professional associations, and develop and maintain professional contacts. By doing so, you will be helping to ensure yourself a satisfying and rewarding future in the dynamic and exciting field of crafts.

RECOMMENDED READING

Brabec, Barbara. *Creative Cash: How to Sell Your Crafts.* Tucson, AZ: HP Books, 1991.

Career Associates. *Career Choices for Students of Art.* New York: Walker, 1990.

Davis, Sally Prince. *Graphic Artist's Guide to Marketing and Self-Promotion.* Cincinnati, OH: Northright Books, 1991.

Dole, Hilary, ed. *Craft Digest.* Northfield, IL: Digest Books, Inc.

Feirer, John L. *Furniture and Cabinet Making: A Complete How-To By America's Foremost Expert.* NY: Scribner, 1983.

_____. *Woodworking For Industry.* Peoria, IL: Bennett Publishing Co., 1979.

Ganim, Barbara. *The Designers Commonsense Business Book.* Lincolnwood, IL: NTC Business Books, 1993.

Gordon, Barbra. *Opportunities in Commercial Art & Graphic Design.* Lincolnwood, IL: VGM Career Horizons, 1992.

Index of Majors and Graduate Degrees 1993. New York: College Entrance Exam Board, 1993.

Kirklighter, Clois E., and Ronald J. Baird. *Crafts.* South Holland, IL: Goodheart-Willcox Company, Inc., 1986.

Knox, Gerald, ed. *Traditional American Crafts.* Iowa: Meredith Corporation, 1988.

McKay, Robert. *Opportunities in Your Own Service Business.* Lincolnwood, IL: VGM Career Horizons, 1987.

McRae, Bobbi A. *The Fiberworks Sourcebook.* White Hall, Virginia: Betterway Publications, Inc., 1985.

Miller, Laurie, ed. *Artist's Market.* Cincinnati, OH: North Light Books, Annual.

Pulos, Arthur. *Opportunities in Industrial Design.* Lincolnwood, IL: VGM Career Horizons, 1988.

Rorabaugh, W. J. *The Craft Apprentice: From Franklin to the Machine Age.* New York: Oxford University Press, 1988.

Rowh, Mark. *Careers for Crafty People and Other Dexterous Types.* Lincolnwood, IL: VGM Career Horizons, 1994.

Seidman, Joel I. *The Needle Trades.* New York: Farrar and Rinehart, 1942.

Sheldon, Roger. *Opportunities in Carpentry Careers.* Lincolnwood, IL: VGM Career Horizons, 1993.

Smith Kern, Coralee. *How to Run Your Own Home Business.* Lincolnwood, IL: VGM Career Horizons, 1990.

United States Department of Labor Bureau of Statistics. *Occupational Outlook Handbook.*

United States Department of Labor—Employment and Training Administration. *Dictionary of Occupational Titles.*

Walker, Linda and Steve Blount. *Getting the Max From Your Graphics Computer.* Cincinnati, OH: North Light Books, 1991.

Wasserman, Paul, and Edmond L. Applebaum, eds. *Festivals Sourcebook.* Detroit: Gale Research Co., 1984.

Weills, Christopher, ed. *The Goodfellow Catalog of Wonderful Things.* Radnor, PA: Chilton Book Company, 1984.

AMERICAN CRAFT COUNCIL

The American Craft Council (A.C.C.) is a national nonprofit educational organization that was founded in 1943 by Aileen Osborn Webb. Mrs. Webb, a potter, was a well-known patron of the arts in the 1930s. Convinced of the need to provide better marketing opportunities to craftspeople, she spent many years developing programs to increase their visibility and sales. The founding of the American Craft Council was the culmination of many years of dedication and hard work.

The primary goal of the A.C.C. is to develop interest in and appreciation for contemporary crafts. Headquartered in New York City, the A.C.C. performs a number of important functions for American craftspeople. It publishes the bimonthly magazine *American Craft,* sponsors the American Craft Council Library, offers a nationwide audiovisual service, and maintains the American Craft Museum. In addition, its subsidiary, American Craft Enterprises, Inc., organizes craft shows and fairs throughout the country.

The American Craft Council Library is an invaluable information center and reference service for craft professionals. The library includes the following information:

- Artists Registry and Archives—with files on more than 200 craftspeople. A list of craft organization membership rosters is also maintained.
- More than 4,000 crafts-related books.
- More than 3,000 catalogs on crafts-related exhibitions.
- Back issues of at least 75 crafts-related periodicals.
- Newsletters of national, regional, and local craft organizations.
- Clipping files on a wide variety of subjects.

Membership in the A.C.C. is open to all. At the present time, a one-year membership costs about $40 ($30 for students and senior citizens) and includes the following benefits:

- Six issues of *American Craft Magazine*.
- Free admission to the American Craft Museum and American Craft Council Library.
- Discounts on A.C.C. publications.
- Eligibility for A.C.C.-sponsored group insurance.
- One free admission to each A.C.C. craft fair organized by American Craft Enterprises, Inc.
- A vote in the A.C.C. annual election of trustees.
- An A.C.C. membership card.

For more information on the American Craft Council and how to apply for membership, write or call the following:

American Craft Council
   72 Spring St.
   New York, NY 10012
   (212) 274-0630

OTHER PROFESSIONAL ORGANIZATIONS

American Association of Museums
  1225 1ST. NW, Ste. 200
  Washington, DC 20005
  202-289-1818

American Ceramic Society
  757 Brooksedge Plaza Dr.
  Westerville, OH 43081
  614-890-4700

American Forestry Association
  1516 P St. NW
  Washington, DC 20005
  202-667-3300

American Furniture Manufacturers Association
  P.O. Box HP-7
  High Point, NC 27261
  919-884-5000

American Historical Society
    400 A Street, SE
    Washington, DC 20003

American Institute for the Conservation of Historical
    and Artistic Works
    1400 16st St. NW, Ste. 340
    202-232-6636

American Scientific Glassblowers Society
    1507 Hagley Rd.
    Toledo, OH 43612
    419-476-5478

American Sewing Guild
    P.O. Box 50976
    Indianapolis, IN 46250
    317-845-9128

American Society of Appraisers
    P.O. Box 17265
    Washington, DC 20041
    703-478-2228

Appraisers Association of America
    541 Lexington Avenue
    New York, NY 10022

Associated General Contractors of America
    1957 E Street, NW
    Washington, DC 20006
    202-393-2040

Counted Thread Society of America
    1285 S. Jason St.
    Denver, CO 80223
    303-733-0196

Crochet Association International
P.O. Box 131
Dallas, GA 30132
404-445-7137

Embroiderers' Guild of America
335 W. Broadway, Suite 100
Louisville, KY 40202
502-589-6956

Gemological Institute of America
1660 Stewart St.
Santa Monica, CA 40404
213-829-2991

Glass Art Society
P.O. Box 1364
Corning, NY 14830
607-936-0530

Glass, Pottery, Plastics, and Allied Workers
International Union
Box 607
608 East Baltimore Pike
Media, PA 19063
215-565-5051

Handweavers Guild of America
120 Mountain Ave.
Bloomfield, CT 06002
203-242-3577

International Guild of Candle Artisans
867 Browning Ave., S.
Salem, OR 97302
503-364-5475

National Association for the Cottage Industry
  P.O. Box 14850
  Chicago, IL 60614
  312-472-8116

National Auctioneers Association
  8880 Ballentine
  Overland Park, KS 66214
  913-541-8084

National Quilting Association
  PO Box 393
  Ellicott City, MD 21043
  301-461-5733

National Woodcarvers Association
  7424 Miami Ave.
  Cincinnati, OH 45243
  513-561-0627

Society of Illustrators
  128 East 63rd Street
  New York, NY 10021
  212-838-2560

Stained Glass Association of America
  4050 Broadway, Ste. 219
  Kansas City, MO 64111
  816-561-4404

United Brotherhood of Carpenters and Joiners of America
  101 Constitution Avenue, NW
  Washington, DC 20001
  202-546-6206

STATE ARTS COUNCILS

Associated Councils of the Arts
  1285 Ave. of the Americas, 3rd fl., Area M
  New York, New York 10019

Alabama State Council on the Arts and Humanities
  322 Alabama Street
  Montgomery, Alabama 36104

Alaska State Council on the Arts
  Fifth Floor MacKay Building
  338 Denali Street
  Anchorage, Alaska 99501

Arizona Commission on the Arts and Humanities
  6330 North 7th Street
  Phoenix, Arizona 85014

Arkansas State Council on the Arts and Humanities
  400 Train Station Square
  Little Rock, Arkansas 72201

California Arts Commission
  808 O Street
  Sacramento, California 95814

Colorado Council on the Arts and Humanities
Room 205, 1550 Lincoln Street
Denver, Colorado 80203

Connecticut Commission on the Arts
340 Capitol Avenue
Hartford, Connecticut 06106

Delaware State Arts Council
601 Delaware Avenue
Wilmington, Delaware 19801

District of Columbia Commission on the Arts
Room 543, Munsey Bldg.
1329 E Street, NW
Washington, DC 20004

Fine Arts Council of Florida
Department of State
The Capitol Building
Tallahassee, Florida 32304

Georgia Council for the Arts
225 Peachtree Street, NW, Suite 706
Atlanta, Georgia 30303

Hawaii—The State Foundation on Culture and the Arts
250 South King Street, Room 310
Honolulu, Hawaii 96813

Idaho State Commission on the Arts and Humanities
P.O. Box 577
Boise, Idaho 83701

Illinois Arts Council
111 North Wabash Avenue, Room 1610
Chicago, Illinois 60602

Indiana Arts Commission
  155 East Market Street, Suite 614
  Indianapolis, Indiana 46204

Iowa State Arts Council
  State Capitol Building
  Des Moines, Iowa 50319

Kansas Arts Commission
  166 West 10th Street, Suite 100
  Topeka, Kansas 66612

Kentucky Arts Commission
  400 Wapping Street
  Frankfort, Kentucky 40601

Louisiana Council for Music and Performing Arts
  611 Gravier Street
  New Orleans, Louisiana 70130

Maine State Commission on the Arts and Humanities
  State House
  Augusta, Maine 04330

Maryland Arts Council
  15 West Mulberry Street
  Baltimore, Maryland 21201

Massachusetts Council on the Arts and Humanities
  14 Beacon Street
  Boston, Massachusetts 02108

Michigan Council for the Arts
  1200 Sixth Avenue
  Detroit, Michigan 48226

Minnesota State Arts Council
  100 East 22nd Street
  Minneapolis, Minnesota 55404

Mississippi Arts Commission
301 North Lamar Street
Jackson, Mississippi 39205

Missouri State Council on the Arts
111 South Bemiston Street, Room 410
St. Louis, Missouri 63117

Montana Arts Council
Fine Arts Building, Room 310
University of Montana
Missoula, Montana 59801

Nebraska Arts Council
8448 West Center Road
Omaha, Nebraska 68124

Nevada State Council on the Arts
560 Mill Street
Reno, Nevada 89504

New Hampshire Commission on the Arts
Phoenix Hall
North Main Street
Concord, New Hampshire 03301

New Jersey State Council on the Arts
27 West State Street
Trenton, New Jersey 08625

New Mexico Arts Commission
State Capitol
Santa Fe, New Mexico 87501

New York State Council on the Arts
250 West 57th Street
New York, New York 10019

North Carolina Arts Council
  Department of Cultural Resources
  Raleigh, North Carolina 27611

North Dakota Council on the Arts and Humanities
  North Dakota State University
  Fargo, North Dakota 58102

Ohio Arts Council
  50 West Broad Street, Room 2740
  Columbus, Ohio 43215

Oklahoma Arts and Humanities Council
  1140 NW 63rd, Suite 410
  Oklahoma City, Oklahoma 73116

Oregon Arts Commission
  494 State Street
  Salem, Oregon 97301

Commonwealth of Pennsylvania Council on the Arts
  503 North Front Street
  Harrisburg, Pennsylvania 17101

Rhode Island State Council on the Arts
  4365 Post Road
  East Greenwich, Rhode Island 02818

South Carolina Arts Commission
  1205 Pendleton Street
  Columbia, South Carolina 29201

South Dakota State Fine Arts Council
  108 West 11th Street
  Sioux Falls, South Dakota 57102

Tennessee Arts Commission
  Room 222, Capitol Hill Building
  Nashville, Tennessee 37219

Texas Commission on the Arts and Humanities
  202 West 13th Street
  Austin, Texas 78701

Utah State Institute of Fine Arts
  609 East South Temple Street
  Salt Lake City, Utah 84102

Vermont Council on the Arts
  136 State Street
  Montpelier, Vermont 05602

Virginia Commission on the Arts and Humanities
  1215 State Office Bldg.
  Richmond, Virginia 23219

Washington State Arts Commission
  1151 Black Lake Boulevard
  Olympia, Washington 98504

West Virginia Arts and Humanities Council
  State Office Building No. 6
  1900 Washington Street East
  Charleston, West Virginia 25305

Wisconsin Arts Board
  107 S. Butler Street
  Madison, Wisconsin 53702

Wyoming Council on the Arts
  200 West 25th Street
  Cheyenne, Wyoming 82002